BONBONS FOR YOUR BRAIN

Books By Diane Vallere

Samantha Kidd Mysteries

Designer Dirty Laundry *Pearls Gone Wild*
Buyer, Beware *Cement Stilettos*
The Brim Reaper *Panty Raid*
Some Like It Haute *Union Jacked*
Grand Theft Retro

Madison Night Mad for Mod Mysteries

"Midnight Ice" Novella *The Decorator Who Knew*
Pillow Stalk *Too Much*
That Touch of Ink *The Pajama Frame*
With Vics You Get Eggroll *Lover Come Hack*

Sylvia Stryker Outer Space Mysteries

Fly Me To The Moon
I'm Your Venus
Saturn Night Fever

Mermaid Mystery Novellas (summer 2019)

Tails from the Deep
Murky Waters
Sleeping with the Fishes

Material Witness Mysteries

Suede to Rest
Crushed Velvet
Silk Stalkings

Costume Shop Mystery Series

A Disguise to Die For
Masking for Trouble
Dressed to Confess

Non-Fiction

Bonbons For Your Brain

diane vallere

 POLYESTER PRESS BOOKS

BONBONS FOR YOUR BRAIN
A Collection of Essays
A Polyester Press Publication

All rights reserved. No part of this book may be used or reproduced by any means, graphic, electronic, or mechanical, including photocopying, recording, taping, or by any information storage retrieval system without the written permission of the publisher except in the case of brief quotations embodied in critical articles and reviews.

First published April 2019

Copyright © 2019 Diane Vallere

All rights reserved.

Paperback ISBN: 9781939197603
Hardcover ISBN: 9781939197641
ebook ISBN 13: 9781939197344

Printed in the United States of America.

For my fellow Weekly Divas

Introduction

The term "Weekly Diva" was an accident. I was looking for a name for my author newsletter and had decided to start sending it weekly. I have always known the J. Lo version of my name is D-Va (phonetically "diva") so I became DiVa.

For a while I considered and discarded the moniker because of the negative connotations, but once I embraced it, I started to love it in an ironic way. I don't feel like a diva. I don't act like a diva. But thanks to the name my parents gave me, I *am* a diva.

In the first year of sending the Weekly DiVa to my readers, I experienced my first major health crisis. A long-term romantic relationship ended. I served as president of a national non-profit, parted with my literary agency, and published my twenty-fourth book. I felt empowered simply by sending an email once a week, an email that did little more than connect me with a group of people I otherwise may never have known existed.

But when a change in lifestyle drove me to more frugal choices, I knew I could take care of myself. Being a weekly diva is not spending wildly or pinching pennies. It's somewhere between the two. It's curating your decisions, choosing to be choosy, and choosing yourself. We may be women every day, but I challenge you to be a diva at least once a week.

Truffles

(FASHION & BEAUTY)

Remembering Yesterday

Fashion is a funny business. No matter how successful an event is—a fashion show, shopping party, annual sale, or unexpected trend like leg warmers—before it's over, you're already worried about how you're going to top those results. Good reviews and big sales numbers are celebrated for only a fraction of a second, almost always followed up with, "What's next?" In short, you're only as good as your most recent success.

The business of fashion is about change, sure, and the "What's Next" keeps it moving forward. Upcoming fashions for spring are already in the past for designers ironing out their visions for next fall. Their long-term vision embraces tomorrow as a fact of life, while looking to the distant past for inspiration.

I have no issues with tomorrow. In fact, I think a belief in tomorrow's potential is what gets most people to their goals.

But what about yesterday?

Maybe in our haste to get what we want, we spend too little time feeling good about what we have. Maybe pausing to savor the small success in our recent past is like stopping to smell the roses, reminding us that everything we want won't happen overnight, but that we're on the right track to get there someday. And when we're in a slump, not motivated to thread a needle that keeps breaking, strategize for next month's big shopping event, or re-edit the manuscript that can't quite get past the gatekeepers of the publishing industry, revisiting recent success might give us what we need to keep going. Maybe, just maybe, we're too eager to trade last year's neon for this year's camel, too quick to give up on legwarmers when they try to make a comeback, too focused on the finish line to see how far we've come since we started playing the game.

Let's face it. The potential for tomorrow is greater because of what happened yesterday. We mostly look forward because we have goals, we have aspirations, and their realization lies in the future. But maybe we need to dig out some forgotten piece of fashion that we kept, not because it's back in style, but because it's connected to the yesterdays that helped define us and get us to where we are today.

Maybe it's time to dig out those legwarmers.

Or maybe not. It's hard to say.

Sweatpants Are Never the Answer

I remember it like it was yesterday. March 20, 1990. The only time in my life (not related to a sporting event) where I was caught in public in sweatpants. And I'm not talking about the chic designer jog suits trend that lurks at the edges of the style spectrum. I'm talking about heather-gray cotton/poly blend with the elastic at the ankles.

I shudder at the memory.

I was planning to sleep out for tickets to Madonna's Blonde Ambition tour. It would be Madonna's and my third tours together. Other tour tickets had been procured by getting up really, really early. But this time, I was prepared for an adventure.

I changed from work clothes to comfy sweat clothes and parked near the Ticketmaster mall door. A few other people dotted the sidewalk with coolers and quilts; at 7 p.m., I wasn't the first in line (but close enough).

Now here's where it gets a little messy. My at-the-time

boyfriend (destined to become an ex, and don't think there's no coincidence) drove to my car and picked a fight with me. One of those "you-don't-have-your-priorities-straight" fights, because I'd chosen sleeping out for Madonna tickets over bowling with his friends. And while maybe the priority thing could be said of me in other instances, this was Madonna. Blonde Ambition. 1990. All things considered, my priorities were straight as the shortest distance between two points.

But this was a relationship still in its relative infancy, and fights happen for a reason. And maybe, just maybe, if I showed this future-ex that he was more important to me than Madonna, we'd get past this. I got out of line, emotionally drained myself through the ensuing forty-something minute long rehash of my priorities, and somehow ended up hanging out with future-ex and his friends that night. In a bowling alley. In sweatpants.

Tim Gunn calls it a Sweat suit alternative. Stacy and Clinton from TLC's *What Not To Wear* call it Chic Mom on the Go. Stylists all over the world have a catch phrase for acceptable, run around, be comfy-but-attractive attire. While they may never agree on whether orange is the new pink, how much leopard print is too much leopard print, or the political implications of low-rise jeans, they agree on this: there is always a better option than sweatpants. Take it.

Do this now. Find at least one outfit that is comfy and cute. A no-brainer. One that can take you anywhere. One that answers yes to these questions:

a) Can you wear it to an unexpected invitation?

b) Can you sleep in it?
c) Can you walk a mile in it?
d) Would it get ruined if it got wet?
e) Can you fight in it? (This point remains untested but seems like good sense.)

When you can answer yes to these five questions, you've answered one of life's most important conundrums. And now you're a little bit closer to peace.

I bought those Madonna tickets the morning after wearing those sweatpants, but the concert wasn't destined to be. Madonna canceled that tour due to a sore throat and refunded the money. She rescheduled for later that summer, but I didn't attend, and I haven't been to one of her concerts since.

It's for the best. I changed a little that night, wearing sweatpants in public. I gave up a piece of myself and could never go back.

Learn from my mistakes, folks. Don't give sweatpants a chance.

It Started with a Chanel Suit

I've been thinking a lot about my writing journey lately, probably because six years ago I published my first book. But before that, before having a book to publish, before getting my very first rejection letter, was a moment I remember clearly. It started with a Chanel suit.

Allow me to provide some background info. When I graduated from college with a degree in fine arts, I, shall we say, lacked direction. I didn't know what life in the grown up world would be like, but it seemed wise to set goals for the future. I set myself three goals to achieve by the time I was forty:

1. Swim the English Channel
2. Run a marathon
3. Own a Chanel suit

Now, while one and two might seem a little out of left field, I should also mention that I'd been a competitive swimmer for fifteen years (that first year, when I was six, was more like playing around in the water), and that my college tuition was funded by a partial scholarship. My specialty was long distance and my niche specialty was open water swims. Yes, it was a stretch, but it wasn't like I pulled it out of a hat. Running a marathon was slightly less within my grasp. I'd been known to run to stay in shape, though the longest I'd managed was seven miles. So more of a stretch than swimming the English Channel, but not entirely outside the realm of possibility.

The suit, well, I've always loved clothes and a Chanel suit is the brass ring of status symbol/quality/out-of-my-reach pipe dream desires.

Fast forward fourteen years. The English Channel swimming and the marathon running were but vague concepts. But I worked in retail management. One of my areas of responsibility was the Chanel salon. And, I had a discount.

Here's the part I remember clearly: one day I was at the store, working on the displays inside the Chanel salon, when it hit me. As expensive as a Chanel suit was, the reason I didn't own one wasn't because I couldn't afford it. My household monthly bills exceeded the cost of a Chanel suit: mortgage, two car leases, cable, credit card debt, cell phones, landline phones, and various other expenses I can't even remember. Every time I'd been promoted at work, my lifestyle had shifted upward and quickly sucked up any of that extra money, which kept me constantly working toward the next promotion almost from the minute I achieved the most recent one. The problem here was I didn't care about any of those things.

I was married to someone with different values than I had. It had always been my joke: I'd rather spend money on shoes than on a car; they're both methods of transportation. But somehow, the car(s), the house, the luxury items, and the aspirational wealth had become my way of life. I had no money of my own because it all went to the other things, including the debt. I'm certainly not the only person who has lived this way, but standing there in the Chanel Salon, surrounded by beautiful clothes that I had always hoped to own, knowing I was at a level where I could afford it yet didn't have the control over my finances to actually do so, I realized something.

If I wrote a book and made money from that book, that would be my own money, and I could spend it however I pleased.

Okay, fine, nobody publishes to make a zillion dollars. But still, the idea that I had something within me that I could do that could lead to my own thing—not something anybody else could claim shared credit for—left me feeling exhilarated.

Shortly after that, I had the idea for Samantha Kidd, former fashion buyer turned amateur sleuth. She gives up her glamorous and successful career in order to move back home and rediscover who she once was and where she got off the track to her own happiness. There's a lot of me in Samantha Kidd, though at the time I didn't realize I'd be following in Samantha's footsteps a few years later.

The Chanel suit came, too.

If you're wondering if I ever got the suit, I did. It was marked down 75 percent, plus my employee discount, and still cost more than the rent on my last apartment. I still have it, I still wear it, and I still love it.

My advice to you is this: it doesn't matter what motivates you. You don't even have to tell people why you're doing what you're doing. But if you're unsettled, if you're looking for a change, if you realize that somewhere along the line you lost your passion, you should do something. Figure out what your carrot is and then dangle it.

Hemming and Hawing

Not too long ago, I had my favorite pair of harem pants hemmed. My goal was to find that sweet spot in length that would work with either a flat shoe or a heel. The fitter pinned the left leg (with me in the heel) and told me they were perfect and left me in the fitting room to admire them while she wrote up the price ticket. I took that shoe off and slipped a flat sandal on and the pants buckled on my instep and covered my heel—not the look I wanted.

(It might be a good time to define harem pants: think *I Dream of Jeannie/ Arabian Nights*, not MC Hammer/ Lisa Bonet in *The Cosby Show*.)

I called the fitter back into the room and she declared again that the length was perfect. I tried to explain that this wasn't your basic wide leg pant, blah blah blah, and that for a harem pant you needed to see the balloon of the fabric. She suggested I get another opinion, which I did. They agreed with the fitter. Once again I launched into my exposition of the harem pant and the stylistic demands of such an item. If I simply wanted a pair of wide legged pants, I would have bought them.

The fitter suggested if I didn't trust myself, that I walk into the store and ask other coworkers. And that's when it hit me. I did trust myself. I trusted my vision. What I didn't trust was the opinion of the other people. I knew what I wanted, what I saw, and what I was trying to achieve.

Oddly enough, this reminds me of the process of writing. A writer finishes a story and, after tweaking and polishing, thinks it's ready for the world. Once you start sending it out to beta readers, family members, or agents, you'll start getting feedback: "I loved the concept," "I didn't connect," "I read it in one sitting!," "It's not right for me." Some people will say, "I wished it had more X." Others will say, "I wished it had more Y." The more people you ask, the more opinions you'll get. And it's easy to get on a rollercoaster of edits, trying to please everyone.

But there needs to be a point where you inherently understand and respect your own vision. What one person can't stand is what another person loves. Know what you're trying to accomplish and trust your instincts. Because some day someone dressed like a genie might show up with a magic lantern and offer you a couple of wishes, and the more secure you are in your own vision, the easier it will be to pursue what you want.

Arguments for and against Buying a Black Leather Fringed Skirt

FOR:
1. When will I ever see an item like this again?
2. The bottom row of fringe comes to mid-knee cap so it is totally age appropriate.
3. May I say again: FRINGES!
4. Wearing it will make me feel like a DWTS contestant about to do the jive/samba/cha-cha.
5. Black goes with everything.
6. It's like Candy Johnson meets Bon Jovi!

AGAINST:
1. It is not cheap.
2. It is one of two black leather skirts that I am considering
3. and the other is more practical.
4. How often can I wear it?
5. It's like Candy Johnson meets Bon Jovi.
6. The fact that I can't come up with five arguments against

purchasing tells me that I might not be viewing the decision with the highest degree of rationality.

You might wonder why I'm debating the merits of a possibly impractical purchase instead of writing, and I'll tell you. Writing is hard work. It's a job, not all fun and games. Writing takes dedication, singularity of focus, and belief in the effort and the goal.

Writing is turning on the muse during random pockets of time, which may be the only times of the day you have to hit your targeted word count. Writing is sending out materials that you believe in for others to judge. Writing is opening yourself up to rejection. Writing is perfecting your craft, taking classes, and revisiting works that have been shelved because you realize you can make them better.

All of this work comes at a price. Your mind is always working and you need some down time. When you work hard at a full-time job, you sometimes get a bonus. You sometimes get a raise. You sometimes treat yourself, spend some of your hard-earned money, simply to reward your own efforts. When you work hard at writing you deserve something, too.

No matter how passionate you are about your job, sometimes you have to let your brain think about something else. Something that doesn't matter as much. Not how you're going to pay the Visa bill or what you're going to make for dinner on Thursday night. Not the mounting library fees from the books you can't seem to return to the library or the mounting pile of laundry that's overflowing from the hamper. Something frivolous.

So whether or not I get the black leather fringed skirt (or

fringed black leather skirt, I can't decide which phrase I like more), for now, it will represent the place where my mind goes when I'm not thinking about advancing the plot, cause and effect, and emotional connection. I still can't tell if frugality and practicality are going to gang up on the fashionista in me and keep me from getting the skirt, but one thing's for sure. Worst case scenario, I'll give it to one of my characters in a future manuscript.

Too Much of a Good Thing?

I took an inventory of my closet the other day and discovered a disconcerting fact. I own over one hundred articles of clothing. And while I'd like to blame this on an archived collection of the best clothes I've ever worn in my life, I gotta be honest. Most of this stuff has been bought in the past five years.

Let's examine the wardrobe first. If I bought it, then I liked it. And if I liked it, then I wore it. But as part of the inventory, I counted how many things I rotate through now, and found that twenty-seven things haven't been worn in over a year. OVER A YEAR!

And shoes. I counted forty pairs. Some of them are like museum pieces (I still love the high-top pink Puma wrestling shoes, even if I never find myself wearing sneakers. And the fact that I own a pair of Jenny-from-the-Block high heeled Timberlands makes me smile, even though you could tip me over if I actually tried to wear them.) and others will be worn out by the end of the year. But still ... forty?

I can't help but think that the things I love are getting lost in the middle of this unit-heavy closet. When news of the recent California fires hit me, and I started thinking about what my own exit strategy would be if I had to get out of Dodge fast. There was a time when my plan was easy: grab the Pucci and the white go-go boots. I could rebuild my life with those two items. But what was my plan now? Grab the Pucci, the white go-go boots, the Mondrian sling backs, the pink patent leather ankle wraps, and the lime green t-straps, and run. Oh, and maybe the black sandals with the white ball heels, and the other black sandals. And my black satin motorcycle jacket. Oh! And my fringed dress!

By now I'd be burnt to a crisp.

Too much of anything can ruin a good thing. Too much wine can ruin a fondue, too much sauce or cheese can throw off the balance of a pizza. Too much styling product can weigh down a great hairstyle, and too many Taylors can cause tension at the heart of Duran Duran.

After finishing my first manuscript, I sent it out on spec to a couple of agents and publishers, convinced it was perfect. More than one suggested it needed to be cut down. I couldn't see how that was possible. I'd lose too many of the words I'd poured my blood, sweat, and tears into. A little time and distance gave me a new perspective, and eventually I took to the delete button and realized my tome was better for the critical edit. The good stuff stood out more. I didn't miss what I deleted. Only after the story was told in its unabridged version was I able to appreciate that less really was more.

Trimming the fat isn't isolated to writing. Watch the deleted scenes packaged on most DVDs and you realize directors consistently have to cut scenes that they love but do little to drive the story forward. You didn't miss those scenes while watching the movie because you didn't know they were once there. And you're only watching the deleted scenes because you liked the final product, right? When's the last time you watched a real stinker and decided to prolong the agony with the special features diskette?

In a nod to the great editorial decisions made by geniuses all over, I'm going to give my closet a critical edit, and get rid of a quarter of my shoes and clothes. I'll invoke the Thoreau mantra to simplify, simplify, and make piles of charitable donations and eBay candidates. Worst case scenario, I'll rack up some karmic points and be more ready to flee in the event of an emergency. Best case scenario, I'll make a couple of bucks.

Either way I'll have room for more stuff, which means I might have to learn this lesson all over again.

Does that make it a series?

Closet Magician

There's a fashion mantra that's been repeated regularly since the concept of dressing for success was introduced, and that is to "Dress for the job you want, not the job you have." For example, I want to be a writer, so I spend a disproportionate amount of time in my pajamas. But recently I had the chance to observe the professional wardrobe of a different career path, that of the magician. And considering I spend a good amount of time trying to get people to believe something that isn't true (I'm talking about writing fiction here!) it seemed only reasonable to examine the importance the wardrobe plays in the success of the professional trickster.

So here, after careful consideration, is my brief, non-scientific, completely subjective breakdown of DRESS FOR SUCCESS, Magician Edition:

1. BLACK SHIRTS: Not T-shirts, but the kind with a collar and buttons down the front. Go for the French cuffs if you

like. Don't be afraid of sparkly cuff links either. The magician is not a wallflower. He may have a few fancy tricks up his sleeve, but that doesn't mean the sleeve can't be fancy, too.

2. FISHNETS: While there aren't as many women in the magic profession (I'm talking headliners, not assistants), the few that I've seen must get a discount on bulk fishnet purchases. I'm thinking it has something to do with diversion.

3. RUFFLES: This one goes both ways. For men, it's the shirt. Think Sonny Bono. Think Liberace. Think James Garner in Maverick. Dye 'em black and you're ready to go. And for the ladies, the ruffles belong on the skirts. Short skirts, too, right above those fishnets, ending at mid-thigh. Again, diversion.

4. COLOR AND PATTERN: Pink blazers. Royal blue tuxedos. Red crinolines. Plaid shoes. Checkered suits. The magician is not afraid to be noticed. In fact, noticing the magician is the first part of his/her act.

5. HATS: Where else do you think the rabbit's going to come from?

What is it about this combination of options that makes it part of the magician's dress code? When smoke and mirrors are tools of your trade, do they cease to be tools of the getting ready process? Or is there a level of freedom that comes with believing in what you are about to do so much that the outfit is merely meant to draw more people to your craft?

The magician's dinner jacket is not unlike a great book jacket in that it makes the audience stop and look for a second. That's the time the magician has to erase the audience's doubts and dazzle them with the show, the moment that most magicians live for. That's why I'm not a magician.

'Cause if it were me, I'd be in it for the wardrobe.

Cashmere Fantasy

Before I started living the glamorous life of the aspiring novelist, I worked at a luxury retailer where I sold fine apparel. We didn't sell things people needed, we sold things people wanted. And being on commission, it behooved me to understand what made people decide to splurge.

Say you walk into the store and pick up a $750 cashmere sweater. It's a lovely sweater, but you've never spent more than seventy-five dollars on a cashmere sweater in your life, and despite its loveliness, you don't understand the price. Why $750? Is that an arbitrary, crazy markup? A mistake?

Enter me. I've been trained in quality clothing and know all about that sweater. I can tell you where the goats that provided the hair that was spun into cashmere live, what part of the goat these fibers are from, and how this is the purest base for cashmere and thus will wear better than other, less-pure cashmere fibers, will pill less, hold color and shape more.

I can explain what the designer was thinking about when he/she chose the shade in your hands. I can tell you what to wear with the sweater, either from your own closet if you choose to tell me about your lifestyle and what you already own, or recommend other items that will complement it. I'll tell you if the sweater is classic or trendy, if the color is right for your complexion, and if it was featured in any magazines recently, on either celebrities or in editorial pages.

It's up to you to listen to what I say and decide if buying the sweater is right for you. And even if you've never spent more than seventy-five dollars on a cashmere sweater in your life, it is possible that if I'm particularly eloquent and witty the day we're talking, if I'm wearing a sassy outfit that you like, if you're intrigued by my stories of Mongolian virgins grooming grass-fed baby goats to extract tufts of cashmere untouched by the sun, or if you walked into my store determined to treat yourself to something extravagant that you might spend ten times your normal cashmere-sweater buying budget and take one home.

That does not guarantee that you won't question your purchase the minute you walked out of my store, or that you won't question the notion of spending more on a sweater than you spend on your monthly car payment. You might even wonder if I knew what I was talking about, although it seemed like I did, and I was witty and eloquent and wearing that sassy outfit...

You might try the sweater on at home, under your own lights, with your own clothes. You might hang the sweater on your bedroom door where it's the last thing you see before falling asleep and the first thing you see upon waking up. You might start to imagine your new life in the sweater, exciting and full of the kinds of opportunities that you wish you had now but you don't. Ultimately you might decide that $750 is too much for you to spend on a cashmere sweater and return it.

That doesn't make what I told you less true. It also doesn't mean you don't deserve the sweater. All it means is that you decided that there are other places you'd rather put your money than into a $750 sweater.

Sometimes indulgences are worth it, whether they are intended to make us feel good or improve our quality of life. It doesn't have to be a $750 cashmere sweater. It could be a professional manuscript edit, a fancy bottle of Champagne, a new hardback book, a memory foam pillow, or a bottle of nail polish. Indulgences remind us that we cherish ourselves, too. And that is sometimes enough to keep us going.

It's All Just a Little Bit of Fashion Repeating

In the words of a former boss and mentor, "Fashion comes around three times in your life, and then you die." It's a weird way to think about your life. It also makes the rehashing of the eighties bittersweet because it means I'm one cycle closer to meeting the Grim Reaper. But now that I've had a chance to witness the repackaging of the eighties, I'm starting to believe that she's right.

I recently watched the TAMI show on public access (*Teenage Awards Music International*). Hosted by Jan and Dean in 1964, it was a live show filled with performances by amazing musicians. The music was fantastic, but I was fascinated by the styles worn by the dancers: skinny Capri pants, deep V-neck sweaters, rugby shirts, and horizontal stripes. And the style of the kids in the audience: shift dresses, pea coats, plaid skirts, turtlenecks, and jackets. It reminded me of high school, twenty years after the show had aired, when I had experimented with my own style with borrowed clothes from my mom's (and dad's) closet which I combined with things I found in second-hand shops and at the mall.

At the time, I didn't understand that the eighties look started because hipsters of the time were shopping in vintage stores for clothes from the forties (much like today's hipsters are wearing clothes from the sixties). They made the look new again: shoulder pads, wide leg pants, menswear, plaid, granny boots. By the time the hipsters influences trickled down to me, it was combined with the mod look of the sixties repackaged, too, i.e. neon, color-blocking, graphic prints. That's what gave the eighties look a life of its own.

So, watching TAMI, it's easy to get lost in the music, but what's really fun is to study the look of the audience. These kids might not have known what was in store for them when they filed into seats in that studio, but they looked like they were ready for anything (except for the girl in the curlers screaming at the James Brown performance. Pretty sure she wasn't quite ready yet). That's how I want to be. Ready for anything. Don't you?

Much like everything else, what was old is new again. Designers continue to pull inspiration from the Eighties, and it's been a trip watching teenagers dress like they raided my 1984 closet. Interestingly enough, I don't want to go there again, though I did love it the first time. Now it's too Been There, Done That. Because even if the Grim Reaper is impervious to the cycles of fashion, I'm still not ready to check the designer label on his robe.

Ode to a Leather Jacket

A few years ago, I was roped into performing a certain hit song from *Grease* at my place of work, which, aside from the fact that I made a complete fool out of myself in front of my peers, was notable for one other reason: I had an excuse to dust off my motorcycle jacket from 1987! In a nostalgic trick taught to me by my mom, the price tag and the receipt are still tucked in one of the smaller pockets. Best $159.99 I ever spent.

I've always been a sucker for a guy in a classic black leather motorcycle jacket. Think Brando in *The Wild One*. Patrick Swayze in *Dirty Dancing*. Adrian Zmed in *Grease 2*. Every greaser in *The Outsiders*. But somewhere around the very wise age of twenty, I realized, instead of looking to meet a guy in a black leather motorcycle jacket, maybe, if I bought the jacket for myself, I'd have one less thing to look for in the guy. So I did.

The jacket became part of my uniform: white T-shirt, ripped jeans, and a mountain of pearls (the late eighties were weird).

Somewhere around the early nineties, the jacket was retired to a closet, unworn but not forgotten. Fifteen years later, when I got a fantastic job and wanted something to commemorate the professional accomplishment, I bought a black satin designer motorcycle jacket which I still wear to this day. It's my own evolution–from the fantasy of the person I wanted to spend my life with, to becoming the person I want to spend my life with.

That's kind of deep, right? And people think fashion is frivolous.

The Power of a Makeover

One of my friends recently told me she felt she was in need of a makeover. She cut and colored her hair, sprung for the foundation for a new wardrobe, and even renovated her office. When she showed me a picture of herself post-changes, my reaction was, "you look completely different!" Which, I'm guessing, was the point.

My friend's personal renovation got me thinking about our collective love of the makeover. Why is the concept of changing our appearance so attractive? Because when we change our appearance, we see something different in the mirror. We no longer see yesterday's failures, but we can imagine tomorrow's successes. For the briefest of moments, when we are literally faced with the shock of change, we are shaken out of our comfort zone into a world of possibilities.

When I left my full-time job, I left behind a generous employee discount, a clothing allowance, and first choice of new sale items, all necessary for the job I was doing. But while leaving that career was an ending, it also represented the beginning of the rest of my life. Did that mean it was time for me to makeover/renovate/shed my skin in order to embrace my new start? When I looked in the mirror, I saw the same person I saw six months ago. Who am I now? Am I the same?

Yes and no. Yes, I'm me. I'm the same person who loves the Go-Gos, owns all the Trixie Beldens, and is drawn to bright colors. But I'm not the person who was tied to the rules of a company anymore. If I wanted to, I could dye my hair blue, drink champagne with breakfast, and wear Moon Boots every day. But just because I can, does that mean I should?

So many of us are looking for our own new beginnings. Some of us are starting a new career. Some of us are retiring from one. Some of us are getting married/ divorced/ having children. Some of us are writing "Chapter One," and some of us are writing "The End." But wherever we are in life, we have a chance to look in the mirror and see the possibilities of the future.

And that is the power of a makeover.

When Good Nail Polishes Go Bad

Two nights ago, I found myself digging through a rather vast collection of nail polishes looking for silver. I know the bottle is in there, but I haven't been in a silver mood since circa 1997, no, wait, I did a silver thing in the early ought's, but it's been shades of pink for about five years now, There it is! Still full, as most of my bottles are, because who actually uses up a full-sized nail polish? I shook the bottle and unscrewed the cap, ready for the first coat (I'd already buffed and top-coated, thank you very much).

But when I extracted the cap from the bottle of futuristic silver, well, there was a problem. The brush was gone!

I stared into the swirling luminescent goo looking for evidence that the brush had once existed. Nothing. It was like the brush had committed some kind of nail polish criminal act and skipped out on the crime scene and nothing short of forensic technology was going to be able to nail that polish brush to the wall.

There was no swaying me from my new silver obsession, so it was time for a Plan B. I dug through the box to find a color worth sacrificing for its brush. But I couldn't open the second bottle; it was sealed shut with its own dried up contents. That's two for two on the Good Nail Polishes Go Bad topic. My older sister recently sent me a box of nail polishes and don't think I didn't wonder if she had sent me a bunch of juvie OPI.

I applied pressure to the handle, heard a minor crunching sound as the interior nail polish walls crumbled, and finally extracted the brush. Cleaned it off with tissues and polish remover and dipped my newly cleaned wand into the space-odyssey-like polish, ready for action. But as I swirled the new brush inside the silver polish, it encountered resistance. I pulled the brush out and found the remains of the former brush. It was as though it had been murdered savagely, its parts scattered under the polish, never to be found. That "bad" brush hadn't committed any crime but had been a victim of its own environment!

Somewhat in shock by what I had discovered, I fished out the rest of the brush and painted my toes on autopilot. I was disturbed that something so pure could become tainted, even when it had only existed in a controlled environment. And because I don't check up on my nail polishes regularly, I didn't know when this happened. Could it have been saved if only I'd paid more attention to it in the last five or so years? Or had that brush been made bad, defective, merely by lurking in the polish, ticking off the days until its untimely demise? Would it have become a victim at the hands of a lesser polish color, say, a delicate shade of pink, or did the silver play a part in its death? Would a color of a different chemical makeup have prolonged its life or encouraged it to fall apart in public?

I'm starting to think that fictitious characters are a lot like nail polishes. You can use them, manipulate them, ignore them, or appreciate them, but you never know what's going on under their surface. And if you assume that what you see is what you get, you're probably not fully experiencing them. Discovering motivation is part of the fun of losing yourself in a good book. It's just another way to say look below the glossy, swirling, super-fantastic, silver pool of polish and discover what lies beneath.

Dark Chocolate

(GOAL SETTING)

On the Road Again

I am no stranger to commuting. For the large part of my working-for-others life, it took an hour each way to get to my job. Two hours a day, five days a week, forty-eight weeks a year ... I did the math. Almost four hundred thousand hours coming and going over twenty years.

My final job was seven miles from where I lived and it took close to an hour to get there. That's Los Angeles, where traffic was as abundant as screenwriters, where everybody was going someplace important and nobody wanted to carpool despite all of the talk about being green. In the same way I've come to accept that I have to do the laundry and wash the dishes, I accepted the commute and joined the chain of cars making the slow crawl down Sunset Boulevard toward Beverly Hills.

But then, things changed. I found a faster way to get from point A to point B.

Like so many journeys, it happened by accident. Traffic was

backed up on my regular route, and in a moment of green arrow-left turn opportunity, I turned onto a residential street. That's when I noticed something unusual. No parking between the hours of 8 a.m. and 10 a.m. Which means, this small residential road was now a two-lane north-south connector between where I was and where I wanted to be. And hardly anybody took it.

I started taking this road regularly and my drive went from fifty-two minutes on average to forty. I saved over ten minutes! That's ten more minutes in bed. Or time to make coffee. Or time to change clothes, to over-accessorize, to reply to a couple of emails, to update my Facebook status.

And like the gift that kept on giving, I discovered my new route got me home faster too. At six o'clock, West Hollywood filled with a mix of people going home and people heading out. Valet stands clogging the right lanes. Never-ending construction causing a backup by businesses taking on renovations. But my new residential road? No restaurants. No valet stands. And the people who lived there parked in their driveways.

Sometimes when you're trying to get somewhere that a lot of other people are trying to get to, too, you get stuck in a clog of traffic. You get behind the woman who applies her makeup at traffic lights. You get behind texting teens and out-of-town business men distracted by their directions. You go this way, because that's the way to get where you're going. It always has been, anyway.

But maybe it's time to try something new? Try a route that isn't so clogged. Just because there are less people on a particular road doesn't make it any less of a road, or any less effective in getting you to where you want to be.

Wasp Work Ethics

There is a wasp living outside of my window. A mud dauber, to be exact. I first noticed her a couple of weeks ago, by the appearance of what looked like a small brown tube about the size of a hollow Bic pen. The tube was attached to the outside of the window casing, and my first thought was: that can't be good.

Removal of a wasp nest is simple: insert a screw driver into the tube and destroy it.

I did not do this.

Over the next several days, I became fascinated with the wasp and her work ethic. What started out as a curious buzzing outside of the window while I was trying to work became a sign that my wasp had arrived and was busy with her own to-do list. Why wasn't I? Every day she showed up and worked steadily on her nest, adding a second small tube of mud, and then a third and a fourth. Every night the tubes were all sealed up, but I could tell which was the most recent by the color of the mud. The next morning, one tube would be open. Did she sleep in there? Was she literally making her bed and then lying in it?

The more she worked, the less I feared her. She was a reminder of what we can accomplish when we wake up and start to tackle a project. Almost anything worth doing takes effort, and we rarely get results overnight. You can't write a book without first writing chapter one, and you can't write chapter one without first writing a first sentence. Producing anything of note—a song, a painting, a sculpture, a book, a poem—requires us to first believe that whatever it is we *want* to accomplish, we *can* as long as we make that first effort.

I've become attached to my wasp. I don't know how much longer she or the nest will be there, but of all the windows around me, she picked mine. I wonder if anybody else would find her actions inspiring. By using spit, mud, and a daily commitment, she's created something. In a way, it's proof that we all have something in us, and if we're willing to get a little dirty and make a little effort, we can create something, too.

Utah

Last Wednesday night, as I was listening to a recap of the fabulous prizes for the winner of Project Runway All Stars, I was struck by one of the items in particular. Not the cash prize. Not the creative suite of technology. It was the one-year position of guest editor for *Marie Claire* magazine. Without thinking too much about it, I said, "That's what I want in ten years. I want to take my 'shoes, clues, and clothes' fashion-themed mystery writing and be successful enough that *Marie Claire* magazine invites me to be a guest editor." I was not alone at the time, and at the look on my companion's face, I followed up with, "What? It could happen."

I should back up and say that being guest editor of *Marie Claire* magazine, or of any fashion magazine, has not been a lifelong dream. It has not been a carefully planned step on a career path, and it does not represent me officially making it. Pretty much, it's something that's far beyond the goals I'm currently striving for, in fact, it kinda dwarfs said goals and makes them look like no big deal.

For a while, the goal was to get a publishing contract. In short, I wanted to be a writer. And while I told myself that writers write, amidst the other things I knew I had to do to achieve the ultimate goal, I did just that. I wrote. But while following the roadmap that had been established by decades of writers before me, the industry changed. It morphed into the Wild West, and my roadmap became useless as I tried to navigate dirt paths and rocky trails, heading toward a place that I didn't quite know how to get to even though I knew it was there.

I stared into the face of opportunity, at the choices of indie publishing vs. vanity publishing vs. small press publishing vs. querying agents, and I froze. The one thing I'd strived for over the course of years, the goal, was now not only within my reach, but it was mine for the taking, if only I was willing to take a chance.

I'll admit I didn't reach for the opportunity and take it. Not at first. I thought about what it would mean to take control of my own writing destiny versus following in the dust trail of thousands of writers before me. I questioned whether I was giving up my dream, whether I was cheating myself out of an experience, whether becoming an indie author was right for me. I took this one little decision and blew it up into something bigger than it needed to be, until it seemed as though everybody I knew had moved on to something while I had tied myself to a railroad track because I couldn't give myself permission to try something else.

I think it's like standing here on earth and staring at the moon, wondering what the moon is like, while there are other people out there who are thinking so far beyond the moon, to what lies beyond the moon. They're not wondering about what's next, but they're wondering about what's after the thing that's after the thing that's after the thing that's next. And by wondering about something so far away, everything else drops into perspective. No one decision is a mistake. It's all forward motion that puts us at a different place on our path, with different opportunities, different choices, and a different career. There's only one thing that the decision does for sure: it takes us to a different place than where we were. And if our goal is to achieve something, to get somewhere different from where we are, then it's important to start making those decisions.

So, I started my own publishing imprint and I treated it like my own little business. I focused on that first book and set a publication date for my second. I looked beyond that first year, setting new goals for where I can be in five and in ten.

Anything–Anything!–can happen in ten years. Don't get bogged down on the decisions you make today or tomorrow. Go with what feels like the right direction. Best case scenario? You could end up in unchartered territory and get the chance to design the exact career you always wanted.

Worst case? You might end up in Utah.

I Did It My Way

I have a pretty effective system when it comes to loading the dishwasher. Wine glasses tilted at an angle on the top row. Plates stacked, small to large, on the bottom, with the cutting board into that very narrow slot at the end. The blender goes into the corner by the flatware bin. The big black roasting pan fits at the back if it's tipped forward, otherwise it gets caught on the top shelf. Like I said, effective.

So when someone else loads the dishwasher, inevitably putting plates and glasses willy-nilly about, I can't help myself. Why did the wine glasses go on the bottom shelf? Why is the big black roasting pan laying face down on the top shelf? Why is the blender in the back? And the slotted spoon is—No! It's chaos! It's anarchy!

Or, it's someone helping me out by loading the dishwasher while I'm otherwise occupied.

I have a hard time asking for help. Perhaps it's because I

want to be independent. Or maybe it's because I think it's an inconvenience. Most likely it's due to that stubborn streak that my sister and I have come to recognize runs in our family. (Hi, Mom! Hi, Dad! Hi, Sis! Waving at you!) But more often than not, if you want to accomplish something, you need to ask for help. And the funny thing is, most of the time people don't mind.

Creativity is a solitary path, but what happens when you're done with your project? You think your manuscript is ready for the world. But is it? Were you typing so fast on page 147 that you missed a word in the middle of a sentence? Did you accidentally leave a note to self on page 75, reminding you to go back and change your red herring to better suit the story? And does that plot twist on page 213 work?

Asking for feedback, for help, is one of the hardest steps for me. I often believe the success of my writing lies in my own efforts. The harder I work, the more serious I am, the closer I'll get. But while writing is a solitary path, feedback is a collaborative effort, and is part of the polishing process. And even the silverware needs a fair bit of polishing after the rinse cycle.

Bottom line: we have to ask for help. We have to find people we trust who can load the dishwasher for us when we're otherwise occupied and know that it doesn't mean we didn't do it all ourselves.

Something Different for a Change

There is a popular notion that if you aren't getting the results you want from the efforts you make, you need to try something different. Let's face it, we all have goals, whether they are getting published, getting a better job, or getting a date for Saturday night.

If we do the same thing over and over and get the same results, we're spinning our wheels. And instead of getting results, we're getting nowhere. Our efforts become an exercise in futility. We're like Sisyphus pushing a boulder up a hill, only to do it again tomorrow. He was dealing with a punishment from the gods, and no matter how he gets that boulder up there today, he's going to be doing it again. And again. And again.

So (assuming we're not being punished by the gods) why shouldn't we try a different tack toward achieving our goals every once in awhile? I toss down the gauntlet of Trying Something Different to you. It doesn't have to be a grand difference. It could be taking a different route to work. It could be shopping at a different grocery store. It could be acknowledging to someone other than the voices in your head (you have those too, right?) what you're trying to achieve.

For me, it was going to the beach.

That's right. Going to the beach.

In the words of the great animated Scat Cat, allow me to elucidate. I used to view a day off during the week as a block of writing time. And I used to use it. Nothing to distract me, a free flow of ideas, time to sit at the computer and hammer out a story . . . priceless.

Yet as I became a full-time writer, my days became routine. They were frittered away with emails and eBay and the other curses of the online E. I lost the focus I had when I only had an hour to write on my lunch break. My writing time barely expanded.

So, I got out of the house. I packed a sandwich and a couple of books and a notebook and pen. My imagination and I set up camp on the sand in front of the ocean where the sun and the sound of the waves fed me.

Who's to say something interesting won't happen, something I can use in the story? I can still come home and have time to futz around on the internet. Worst case scenario, I'll have spent the day at the beach. And that right there is a pretty nice incentive.

I challenge you to find a small difference in the way you approach your goals. Best case scenario? Maybe you'll succeed.

But I Don't Wanna!

I don't wanna clean the apartment.

I don't wanna write my blog today.

I don't wanna do the laundry.

(Can't I just buy clean underwear instead?)

The I-Don't-Wanna mantra invades my life often. It reminds me of a part in my favorite book of all time, *The Phantom Tollbooth* by Norton Juster, where Milo gets caught in the Doldrums.

Case in point: Shortly after waking up today, just like every day, the internal negotiations began. If you know what you're going to wear, you can sleep for an extra five minutes. But if you get up now you'll have time to check your emails before writing. But the bed is so cozy . . . . There are waffles in it for you if you get up THIS SECOND. Coffee, too. Okay, buy coffee later and stay in bed for one more minute. Okay, no waffles, stay in bed for two more minutes. Okay, get up at exactly the moment when the second hand hits the twelve. Now! Or in another minute. Just one...

It's not that I don't have things to do. It's simpler than that; I was comfortable. I didn't want to get out of bed.

The problem with being comfortable is that it is often at odds with being productive. When I get up earlier than I need to, I gain extra time to write, and that is the most absolute fun thing that I do in the course of a day.

In a past life, I was a competitive swimmer. I had early morning practice several days a week. I didn't want to get up then either, but I did. It was dark, cold, and lonely. There were days when I was the only person in the pool. I hated morning practice. HATED IT. But if I didn't do it, chances were that somewhere out there in a different dark, cold, lonely pool my competition was, and they'd have an edge. So I did it, because it was important to me.

Didn't mean the I-Don't-Wannas weren't there. (I definitely didn't want to dive into 68-degree water at 6:30 a.m.!)

I think about this now, not the act of swimming in the morning, but the idea of using the time available to be better at what is important. I don't wanna get up early to write, but when I do, I increase my word count, or start the creative juices flowing so it's easier to work through the tough spots. I send out query letters or request materials. I edit a rough patch, or I start/finish a synopsis for an upcoming project. Bottom line is, though I don't wanna, I do. And when I do, I am always pleased with the result, even if the result is minimal. Why? Because it's important to me.

But the I-Don't-Wanna's aren't going to stop.

I don't wanna save money for a rainy day. (When exactly is this "rainy day?" Is it any rainy day? The next day it rains, do I get to spend whatever I've saved?)

I don't wanna send out a proposal that might turn into a rejection.

But I know what I *do* want. When the I-Don't-Wannas whisper in my ear, I mentally inject a dose of anti-toxin. I remind myself what's important to me.

Anatomy of a Goal

After years of aspiring to the traditional model of success for being published, I started wondering if there was another way to reach my goal. Even if you're not following publishing industry news daily, you've probably heard of store closings and you probably know someone with a Kindle or a Nook, so you are at minimum slightly aware that something has changed in the book buying/book reading world.

So, it's time to revisit my goals and try to figure out how to stay on that yellow brick road that winds around quite a bit but hopefully will take me where I want to go. Here's how my internal monologue plays out:

PROSPECTIVE GOAL: I want to be published.

INTERNAL RESPONSE: Weren't you recently published in an anthology?

OKAY. REVISED PROSPECTIVE GOAL: I want an agent.

INTERNAL RESPONSE: Would the fact of signing with an agent be enough? What if said agent never sold any of your projects? Would the validation of having an industry pro believe in what I write be enough?

FINE. REVISED, REVISED PROSPECTIVE GOAL: I want people to find/buy/enjoy my books.
INTERNAL RESPONSE: That's a crap shoot. All you can control is writing the best books that you can. There will be people who love it and people who don't. That is important. In fact, you better start chanting that to the mirror every morning.

(Let's check the attitude, shall we?)

GRRR. REVISED, REVISED, REVISED PROSPECTIVE GOAL: I want to have actual books to sell and sign at fun events.
INTERNAL RESPONSE: How long are we going to do this? (Besides, you're the one who's being difficult.) Figure out what you want and what you can control and do that.

Is it really that easy? Yes.

No matter how carefully you word your goals, you won't achieve them until you get into motion.

Tough Love

When I was a competitive swimmer, I had a coach who was tight-fisted with his compliments. More to his style, he would tell me when I *wasn't* working hard enough to reach my goals. "Vallere, you'll never win the River Swim with practice times like that," still rings in my ear, or even the less popular, "If you're okay letting Competitor X beat you, then keep practicing like that." (He didn't really call her Competitor X, though that would have been cool—like an episode of Speed Racer!) The sad truth was that I didn't want to work out that hard Every. Single. Day. It was tough. And there were times when I wanted to phone it in (and there were probably times that I did, though I will neither confirm nor deny it).

What my coach's words provided were a gauge of my desire to succeed. He didn't tell me I wasn't working hard enough. He dangled the goal in front of me and said that, to get there, I had to make an even bigger commitment than I was doing.

I practiced a lot. Mornings. Nights. Several hours each day. Year after year after year. Swimming was a part of my life (as was the constant smell of chlorine). I wasn't good from the start, but eventually I found my strength. And from that point on I had an even clearer vision of what races I would compete in, who my competition was, and what I could do to gain an edge vs. them (knowing that most of them were wondering the same thing about me).

There was something else my coach did that went hand in hand with his gruff style. When I did well, and I mean *really* well, he relaxed his tough coach exterior and congratulated me. He'd shake my hand and tell me he was proud of what I'd accomplished. Again, he took no credit for pushing me to a place where I could do it, only congratulated me on what I'd done. The good and the bad, he let them be my efforts to accept. He taught me how much control we have over achieving our own goals and aspirations.

I rarely swim anymore but the mindset of practicing to achieve something is set in stone inside my head. And just like those days striving toward a goal in the pool, I'm working toward goals now. Many of us are. And yet we all have days when we don't want to work that hard, days when we wonder "what's the point?"

The next time that hits you, think of what could be if you keep on going. No goals are achieved overnight, but in time, with the right efforts, you can close the distance between where you are and where you want to be.

The Waiting Place

I spent this morning prepping an entry for an online contest that opens today. Yes, I am a self-proclaimed procrastinator. But no, I didn't wait until the last minute to prepare my virtual entry. Yes, I changed my mind this morning about which of my projects I wanted to enter. And no, I wasn't completely prepared with the one I ultimately chose. After writing a new email draft and revamping my pitch, I sat with the computer's clock opened so I could watch the second hand move oh so slowly around in circles until noon arrived and I could click Send.

And, knowing how popular this contest will be, I imagine writers all over doing the same thing. Watching the clock. And waiting.

You wouldn't expect this to be such a big part of the creative process, but it is. Waiting for the muse to strike. Waiting for responses from critique partners, agents, editors. Waiting for Godot. We've been here before; I recognize that tree.

But still, the waiting. How I dislike the waiting.

More and more we're told that if we want to succeed, we have to take ownership of every element relating to our success, and I'm not just talking about writing here. Just Doing It isn't enough. There are Do-ers everywhere, but drive is only one part of the equation. Drive can get you to push a square peg through a round hole, but it will take a lot of effort on your part. Knowledge can teach you how to make the square peg round. Patience tides you over if the sander isn't readily available. The equation of success now contains several components, and unfortunately waiting is one of them.

In *Oh! The Places You'll Go!* Dr. Seuss advises us to avoid the waiting place. That seems like good advice. And, as it turns out, the seven minutes that I waited with hand hovering over my email draft, were for naught–only the first twenty entries received made the contest and I wasn't one of them. My morning of waiting was just that.

But! I did polish the opening of this particular manuscript into something I think is stronger than it was. And I wrote a logline that captures the essence of my mystery. And I did end up with the subject for this essay. All for naught? I think not.

If It Were Easy, Everybody Would Do It

I like to think that it's the perseverance toward a goal that makes a difference, not any particular split-second moment. And that's a pretty good way for me to think, considering I'm not a detail-oriented person and probably cause myself more of an uphill battle than most.

Take this past week (seriously take it and let me have a do-over, because I really, really need it). I knew, have known for awhile, that I had to get a manuscript postmarked by November 30th to be considered for a specific contest. And while it should come as no surprise to anyone who knows me that I'm a procrastinator, the fact that I found myself dealing with my submission at the last minute is not completely due to lack of foresight.

My flash drive, with the version of the project that I intended to send, went kaput two days ago

Now, I am nothing if not resourceful, so I Plan B'd the

contest and chose a different manuscript to submit. But, a corruption in the file had wonked out the formatting, which now needed fixing, and because I'd used up a substantial portion of paper printing out the original choice, I ran out. Black ink, too. I went to Staples.

Or I tried to, because my garage door opener wouldn't work. After thirteen minutes of cursing, clicking, and some general physical activities that make head bangers look like amateurs in a children's play, a neighbor showed up and delivered me to freedom.

In the end, I made the deadline.

If this journey was a sprint, the race would be over before I even got started. And when I think about the mistakes I've made along the way, I could very easily feel like I've self-sabotaged my journey and want to give up. But a very astute person pointed out to me yesterday that life itself is a journey. And every part of it, the good and the bad, is part of the experience. It's all part of the game: the ticking clock, the submissions and rejections, the contests, critiques, opportunities, and closed doors. If you really, really want something, you'll keep trying and keep improving. There's no guarantee that you'll ever see the finish line, but somehow just being in the game can be thrilling.

Flute Lessons

I took flute lessons in grade school, and I imagine that when I was starting out, I was like every other grade-school instrument-playing kid: a challenge to the patience of my instructor. My lessons took place once a week, during the school year, and the practice I invested in learning my craft from week to week was, let's just say, minimal.

But I remember one lesson particularly well. It was the first lesson of a new school year, and my instructor showed up prepared to withstand whatever notes I cared to substitute for B-flat for the next half-hour. She pulled out some sheet music, I positioned my flute, and I played it. Well.

Meaning, I played her selection well.

The best part, at least in my memory, was the look on her face, a combination of surprise and disbelief. I got the impression that she had not expected me to show such growth over the span of a mere three months (considering I'd never shown growth over the span of the nine months that preceded those three). She asked what had happened, and I think my answer was genius in its understatement. "I practiced," I told her.

The reality that I failed to share with my teacher was that one of my closest friends, a year younger than I was, studied the French horn. During that summer, I went to her house and listened to her pull out her horn and play. A tone-deaf Saturday night karaoke singer could tell she was good. Very good. A heck of a lot better than I was.

I didn't mind that she was better at playing French horn than I was at playing the flute. What I minded was that her performance showed me that I could be better. I strengthened my resolve, practiced daily, mastered the fundamentals I should have mastered long ago, and impressed my teacher with unexpected growth when our lessons started back up.

I learned something that summer. I learned that we control how well we do what we do and that competition isn't always about being better than somebody else. Sometimes it's about recognizing our own potential when we see the potential in others.

These days I have different goals, as do my closest friends. Watching them pursue their own goals, though slightly dissimilar to my own, motivates me to work harder to get where I want to be.

And maybe, just maybe, when we all reach our final destination, we can form a band. Dibs on the tambourine—my flute playing is a little rusty.

Waiting to Be Perfect

Over the weekend, I spent some time chatting with a friend who is a singer. We compared notes on the creative process and an interesting concept came up—the idea of not trying to succeed because you're not quite ready yet. Your talent isn't refined. Your work isn't polished. Your ideas are too abstract. You're not yet perfect.

I'm all for trying to improve, but there comes a time when we have to jump off the bridge. We have to recognize that we worked hard to do what we're doing. We applied our natural talent and, maybe we're not yet perfect, but maybe we won't be perfect without input. Feedback. Reaction to what we did. Maybe our first efforts won't be our best and that's okay because we're trying something.

There are people who always wanted to be a writer/painter/poet/artist. And there are people who do these things in the solitude and privacy of their lives, keeping their hand close to their chest. Two different steps along the same path. You have to recognize what you want to do before you do it. But what comes next? Telling people that you created something? Showing them? Asking for criticism?

Or is it better to wait until you've polished your lump of coal so much that it's become a diamond?

Waiting to be perfect discounts the best part of creativity: the joy it provides to simply create something. There are times when I reread portions of a manuscript that I'm writing and I don't remember writing them. It's like the shoemaker's elves took a brief hiatus and cranked out a couple of chapters for me in the middle of the night. But I did write those parts! I did make it up! And that gives me such joy that I want to keep going. I want to know what's coming out of my head next. I'm doing, rather than waiting. And with each time I try, each time I do, I get better.

Don't wait to be perfect. Just start. It feels good. And if you're scared to try, scared to jump off that bridge, then find yourself a like community of people jumping off just like you. I hear those things are easier when done in a group.

I Might Fall Down, but I Get Up Again

I had a situation at work yesterday. In short, the heel of my left shoe got caught in the bow on my right shoe in the middle of a stride. I face-planted into a wall, righted myself, and continued talking to a customer about fabric as though the whole event didn't take place. But it did take place, and I have the broken shoe to prove it. It was embarrassing and awkward and, most tragically, not the first time I've done something of the sort.

I'll go ahead and say it: I am a klutz. For your consideration:

1. BEVERLY HILLS: in an attempt to get more exercise, I started parking a mile from work and walking in. My left foot got caught in the hem of my harem pants while I was stepping off a curb in the middle of the street, and I went down on the asphalt.

2. HOLLYWOOD: walking to the Egyptian Theater, running slightly behind schedule. One block from the theater, in

my Pucci dress and pink Louboutins, I went down on the sidewalk, pretty darn close to Eartha Kitt's star on the Walk of Fame.

3. SUNSET BOULEVARD: On an early trip to Hollywood, I actually slipped on a banana peel that someone had tossed on the sidewalk. You read that right.

4. SOLVANG: walking along a no-traffic street in comfortable wedge sandals. Not a single thing in sight to obstruct my path. I simply fell down.

5. VENTURA: see SOLVANG.

What's the point? Aside from outing myself as a potentially embarrassing/attention-getting walking companion, it's simple: I fall down. I get up. I keep going.

If you think about it, you realize it's not that different from life. We might not all fall down literally, but we get knocked down all the time. Rejection, heartache, loss, failure. Every one of these takes us down a peg, sometimes merely throwing us off kilter but often making us have to start all over again. It's adversity. And once you acknowledge how you act in the face of adversity, you know how to go about moving forward. One step at a time.

70% Pure Cacao

(MENTAL HEALTH)

The You that You Show to the World

One of the more challenging goals of being a writer is the idea that you have to figure out your brand identity and present it to the world. To a business, that's one thing. Consider insurance companies. You might be pulled toward Geico because of the gecko or Progressive because of Flo. Each one of these companies presents a brand image to sell the same product: car insurance at a good rate. I haven't done a comparative study between them to know which one is the best, but I do carry car insurance. So based on what they present to the world, I've made my decision.

But creating a brand image for a person is a little trickier, or at least a little more self-indulgent. I can look at famous people and appreciate the brand they sell: Drew Barrymore, for example, has done a bang-up job. If I go to a Drew Barrymore movie, I know what I'm going to get, and I get it. The same can be said for Adam Sandler, he draws a different audience. Wait, I forgot about

50 First Dates and *The Wedding Singer*. I guess you can say that, at times, two brand images can come together and coexist, introducing each to a new audience. It's like Libby's pumpkin pie mix and Carnation evaporated milk. Madonna might have been the first person I ever realized had branded herself.

Let's say you call yourself some kind of expert of Kaiju. You can wax poetic for hours about Gamera and Odo Island but you're not even aware of Russ Tamblyn's performance in *War of the Gargantuas*. You don't own a single Godzilla T-shirt and there are no aurora models on display in your place of residence. Once you proclaim that Kaiju is part of your identity, how much of it must you not only incorporate internally, but what must you project outward for the world to see as an endorsement of your specialty? If someone followed you around for a week with a hidden camera, would they out you as a fraud?

No matter what you want out of life, you can benefit from figuring out your brand image. Shows like *What Not to Wear* focus on taking a poorly styled person and creating the exterior to match the person inside. They're working with the person's own internal brand image.

What's so Bad about a Mid-Life Crisis?

Several years ago, someone told me I was having a mid-life crisis. Needless to say, I was not pleased by the comment. I was still in my thirties at the time. And, aside from the crushing insult that my life-decisions were little more than a cliché, that would project my full-life span to be somewhere around sixty years old, and I plan to live WAY longer than that. A palm reader once told me I'd live to be ninety-one, and I'll cling to that prediction until I turn ninety (then I'll slowly go crazy wondering how my mortality will end, but I've got years, DECADES, before that becomes an issue).

But a mid-life crisis? Let's break it down.

Mid-life implies that you are halfway through your life. The view backward at your memories is as long as the possibilities ahead of you in your unchartered future. Your life vision encompasses all of the experiences you've had. Can you remember every single thing you've been through? Sure, you remember the highlights, but lots of things will slip through the cracks of memory. If you're mid-life–at the all-important halfway mark—then you can't possibly imagine every single thing that's going to happen to you. Mid-life is like a half-full glass. You may have gone a long way, Baby, but you've still got a long way left to go.

Now let's look at crisis. I'll turn to the experts at Webster for this one: *the turning point for better or worse in an acute disease or fever.* Hmmm. That makes the whole mid-life thing become the disease or fever. Not sure I like that. Let's read on: *a paroxysmal attack of pain, distress, or disordered function.* What? Next: *the decisive moment (as in literary plot).* That one's not bad. Lastly: *an unstable or crucial time or state of affairs whose outcome will make a decisive difference for better or worse.*

Isn't that like every single day?

I don't know about you, but when I start my day, everything's crucial. What am I going to wear? What to pack for lunch? Should I go straight or curly? Bagel or cereal for breakfast? Write at home or the library? How to navigate around that sightseer van that just hit the brakes because the driver wants his paying audience to think they might see a celebrity hanging around Sunset Boulevard?

While those might not be the best examples of unstable or crucial times, they represent the day-in/day-out nature of my life. And who's to say that the mid-life crisis part knocks on the front door and says, "today's the day you're going to have an unstable and/or crucial time on which your future depends." Am I right?

Most of us have a routine, and if we follow it, the unstable and/or crucial time will look like all the other times. Life doesn't change, we do. And think of the second part of that crisis definition: "whose outcome will make a decisive difference for better or worse." That's your kicker, right there.

So, what we're talking about is an unstable and/or crucial time halfway through our lives where the outcome of what happens will make life different either better or worse. You benefit from a pull forward and backward, to the person you've been and the person you want to become, and if there is a riff in the space-time continuum, you are jolted into seeing the reality that where you are isn't where you want to be. And better yet, you're only mid-way through your life, so you've got as much time to change the direction of where you're going as you did getting there. What's so bad about that?

If the first part of your life is following the rules, guidelines, and suggestions of others (parents, teachers, coaches, bosses), then the latter half is about making it up as you go along. Suddenly, you're responsible, in charge of your own destiny. That's a very freeing concept.

I'm starting to think that somewhere along the way the mid-life crisis got a bum rap. Don't you?

If Age is a State of Mind, hy Do My Joints Crack When I Stand Up?

I have been told I don't look my age. I've also been told I don't act my age. But lately, my body has made a point of reminding me that I *am* my age. If I were to stand up right now, something would snap, crackle, or pop. Maybe all three. And the problem is, there's not a darn thing I can do about it.

There are moisturizers that promise the appearance of younger looking skin. Exercises that tone and tighten out-of-shape muscles, and undergarments to do the same thing for those who don't like exercise. We can dye our hair, bleach our teeth, get Botox and microdermabrasion. We can wear clothing that is not age appropriate while listening to Justin Bieber. But at the end of the day, aren't we who we are for a reason? And doesn't that make us the one person that only we can be?

And what's so wrong about that?

I sometimes think about all the energy I've spent trying to be someone I wasn't. This isn't isolated to me either. I know people who are so caught up in projecting the image of success that they are consumed with inevitable fatigue from propping up the lie. There is no shame in being yourself no matter where you are in life.

I've been known to dress in costumes—literal costumes—at public events, and ironically I felt more in touch with myself in a clown tie or safari outfit than dressed to fit in.

I wonder if this is nature's way of reminding us to stretch ourselves. I'm talking about extending ourselves, far beyond what we *think* we can grasp, toward our full potential. Not losing sight of what we once wanted, but twisting and turning, adjusting our posture a little, craning our necks to see around the obstacles that cropped up along the way, working out the kinks in our progress.

Go ahead and reach for the stars. Aside from a little snap, crackle, and pop, what's the worst that can happen?

I Don't Believe You

A funny thing happened on the way to the here and now. Everybody became an expert in something. When's the last time you had a conversation when someone not only listened to what you had to say, but one-upped you with more information? And what happens when you actually *do* know, with some certainty, something about the subject and recognize the BS in your presence?

I like to think of it as the Wikipedia Syndrome. Information is presented in a somewhat convenient forum. It looks very official, and user friendly to boot. What's not to love? Well . . . the fact that, along with valid information, a lot of not-completely-accurate stuff was not so much info as it was a bragging point among the people writing and posting it. I've heard more than once the advice that, if you confirm your facts on Wikipedia, you better confirm them at least two other places before you know you're on solid ground.

The flip side of this is something I rather like–the ability to know what you're talking about as long as you are not having a face to face conversation and you have immediate access to the internet. Yes! The Expert-Badge-For-Everyone! (or EBFE!, which I thought would make a much better acronym when I first typed it out) can eliminate those awkward moments when one person makes a joke and the other doesn't quite get it on a timely basis. As long as you're not in a f2f situation.

But how far will fake expert-dom go? Do we all have an overwhelming need to show off what we've picked up along the way, to the detriment of learning what others can share with us? Can we exchange information in a conversation, a two-way, with two people learning from each other, or has dialogue become like a game of Pong where all we're doing is waiting for the digital ball to come at us so we can lob it back across the screen at the other player?

And the real question is, how comfortable are we at interrupting this new version of Pongversation with the phrase, "I don't believe you?" Because that is the true way to remove the information one-upmanship from a conversation and force it back into the here and now of who knows what.

It's okay to not know everything. It's actually healthier to continue to learn new facts every single day than to pretend to be Mr. Know-It-All. Why, did you know that the pursuit of knowledge burns calories?

You don't believe me? It's true. Look it up on Wikipedia.

Jumping the Battery

If you've ever had a dead battery, then you've found yourself needing a jump. If you left on a light overnight, it's possible that jump will fix your problem. But when your battery dies, no amount of jumping and driving will restore it.

My last car was pretty reliable, but when the battery died, it *died*. I jumped it, but the next morning it was dead again. I bought a portable battery jumper at Pep Boys, and so began a daily ritual of trying to start the car, having a dead battery, and jumping it.

You can see from this story that it isn't my natural inclination to deal with problems head-on. This essay isn't about that character flaw.

The dead battery made me start to think. Why did the battery stop working all of a sudden? What made it go kaput? And why, when I jump it and drove, did it not recharge itself like I was told batteries did?

When I stopped wondering literally about the dead battery in my car, I started wondering figuratively about the battery inside each of us. How do we jumpstart that when it needs a boost?

Let's switch gears. There is some narcissism involved in trying to sell something that you created, because you're the person who came up with the idea, you're the person who took that vision and made it into something, and you're the person who is telling the world at large that it is worth their attention and money.

The fact that you, the sum total of all of the experiences that have occurred in your life, have produced this work, whether it be writing, painting, music, or any other creative endeavor, means your creative battery was charged. And if you did it once, you have to believe you can do it again. But what happens if that battery dies and you can't restart the creativity?

I think we should all take time to expose ourselves to the same things that defined us back when we were in the process of being defined. What music did we love in high school? What books did we devour as a child? What was our routine when we were fifteen? What elements combined to make us the people we are today?

Experiencing these once-familiar things with a fresh perspective will give us a jolt stronger than the stuff you buy in a soda can.

Take some time to jump your battery every now and then. You never know what you'll get out of it once it's gotten a fresh charge. We are never depleted. Our talents don't go away. Why, just two weeks ago I got the idea for a new novel that, well, it's still a work in progress but I'll just say: Time Travel plus Lime Green Boots. Seriously, I can't make this stuff up.

    Oh yeah, I guess I can.

Feminism and Freaky Bugs

I used to think feminism was about equal opportunities. Equal rights. Equal pay. I didn't know it was about killing bugs.

Last night when I went into the bathroom to wash off my makeup, I noticed a weird bug hanging out on the baseboard. Just sitting there, waving some kind of freakishly long tentacles over the slippers that were right below him. I hopped out of the room and pulled the door shut behind me and said, "There's a weird bug in there!" The only other person in the apartment, who happens to have an X and a Y chromosome, took a peek at the bug and confirmed its weirdness. "Yep, that's a weird bug all right," he said, and advised me to kill it.

I guess that wasn't such a novel idea, because that's what I wanted him to do.

So, armed with a relatively full bottle of Oxygen Power, finger on the spray trigger, I opened the door back up and peeked at where the bug resided. He hadn't moved. "Just be quick about it because they move fast!" said the voice behind me.

At this point I may or may not have wished I had a time machine that transported me to the fifties when (I think) it was okay to ask a man to kill a weird bug for you. But no, I wanted the equal opportunities, the equal rights, the equal pay. The entirety of feminism hung over my head. I had to be the one to deal with the bug. Otherwise, I'd be a hypocrite.

I took a deep breath and pulled the trigger, sending a spray of Oxygen Power directly on the bug. Something moved; I didn't wait around to see what. I stepped back into the hallway with the door shut behind me and listened. And watched the gap below the door for signs that the bug was mounting a counter attack.

Ten minutes later, I couldn't stand not knowing what was happening on the other side of the bathroom door. I cracked it open and looked inside. The weird bug was upside down on the slipper. That was a good sign. Upside down bugs usually are dead bugs. But I wasn't taking any chances. That bug was going down. As in, the toilet.

I picked the slipper up off the floor and turned 180 degrees, arm extended, eyes on the bug carcass. Mid-way through my pivot he twitched. OMG! He was playing dead, and now here I was without my Oxygen Power, and he was going to pull a fast one! I flicked the slipper toward the toilet, the bug landed on the inside of the bowl right above the water line, and I swear on the fabulous boots I bought on eBay last week that he started crawling up the side. I hit the flusher and he was carried away in a sea of swirling water. It was over. I'd handled the crisis myself. Gloria Steinem would be proud.

There were no signs of Freak Bug when I got up this morning. There were, however, signs of a slightly more confident tough girl writer spit-shining her double X chromosomes.

Photo Finish

I know of two different photographers who specialize in portraiture. Photographer A's specialty is capturing a person's personality, capturing their essence. She specializes in head shots. Photographer B captures a person's image and retools it, adding a more sculptured cheekbone here, airbrushing off wrinkles there, layering in special effects. In short, A specializes in bringing out the energy on the inside and B specializes in covering up the flaws that are on the outside. There's no question that both photographers are talented. But thinking about each of their approach to their art got me to thinking about vision in general. In short, when you look at something, do you see what is special that is already there, or do you see the flaws?

I think it's human nature to focus on flaws, and to wish they could be taken away. But when I compare the work of these two photographers, I can't help seeing the vitality in Photographer A's photos. Her subjects seem free, alive. And the subjects in Photographer B's works are lifeless but perfect, like ceramic bowls, fragile and still.

So how do we go about seeing ourselves from the perspective of Photographer A's point of view? To see what is good about us, not what's bad? If we focus on our weaknesses, we'll see ourselves as weak. But if we focus on our strengths . . . you can see where I'm going with this, right? Self love and acceptance are as important to our well-being as exercise.

Can we apply it to all aspects of our lives: ourselves, our writing/painting/music/voice? Once we learn to see the intrinsic positives to what we do and who we are, won't the opportunity areas align with that vision and become less of an issue and easier to work with?

It's worth thinking about at least. Take some time to focus on what makes you unique and build upon that. Don't hide your own talents behind a wall of false perfection. Nobody wants to see themselves as underdeveloped.

Fish out of Water

I was a fish out of water in college. As one of the students who made up the 30 percent out of state contingency, I was immediately aware of the vast differences between Virginians and Pennsylvanians. I was a neon and camouflage wearing freshman amongst a whole lot of plaid. My roommate and I, paired by the college's computer, kept a list on the wall of the things we had in common (there were seven). To the majority of the people at the college, I talked funny ("soda" and "you guys" vs. "pop" and "y'all") and I dressed funny (see "neon and camouflage" above). Not a recipe for immediate popularity or acceptance.

I'm not going to lie. After my first semester, I wanted to drop out. I wanted to move home. I wanted to revisit the other colleges on my list, those in New Jersey, Delaware, New York, and Pennsylvania. I wanted to be around people like me. I wanted to be closer to home.

I wanted to belong.

The deciding factor in me attending the college of William and Mary had to do with a swimming scholarship. The college wasn't the highest profile school for swimmers, but they needed a long distance person on their team and that's what I swam, so that, combined with my above-average-but-not-by-much grades from high school gained me admission to the college, and to a community.

Being a part of that swim team kept me going. I made friends, other oddballs like me (my two closest friends and I joked that we were three Milk Duds in a barrel of chocolate covered raisins). The swim team practiced together for hours a day, cheered alongside of each other at meets, traveled in the van to training trips, and partied together after hours. We were a family of sorts.

Williamsburg became a little less lonely for me. My social circle expanded, but the swimmers remained the people who understood me the most. And now, more than twenty-five years after graduating, I remember the camaraderie we shared more than anything else from my college years. That's the power of community: finding and surrounding yourself with a network of people who get past the you-guys and the y'alls, the pops and the sodas, the neon and the plaid, and see you for who you are.

Nougat
(CHEW ON THIS)

Unboxing Barbie

I'm not embarrassed to admit that I have long been a fan of Barbie. I worked in the fashion industry, and while that doesn't make it a given, it doesn't make it a surprise, either. I have fond memories of sitting by the side of Crestwood pool, dressing up my dolls for whatever occasion were deemed the activities of the day. These are the clearest memory that demonstrate my early interest in apparel.

Several years ago, Mattel introduced a new line of collectible Barbies. I was the lingerie buyer for a high fashion specialty store at the time, and the first in the series was the Lingerie Barbie, and, well, I couldn't NOT own her. In both blonde and brunette. It was the beginning of a collection.

Those two dolls were perfection, packaged in a long white box, nestled in filmy tissue paper that was secured with a gold ribbon and, because of a typo on the front of the box that the Mattel team didn't catch before the production run, the dolls skyrocketed in value–shooting to upwards of ten times their purchase price within the first few months. I tucked them away in a closet, knowing they were there, but I dared not look at them too often lest I somehow affect their intrinsic value. I occasionally added a new one to the lot, but that's where the collection remained for years. Tucked away in the closet.

Then one night, while I was packing for a trip, a pipe burst in my hall closet and icky, mucky, smelly water from the air conditioning unit spilled down over my belongings. The Barbies got tsunamied. As fast as I could, I pulled things out to survey the damage. Sure enough, the boxes were destroyed.

I'm not going to lie. Tears were shed.

But then a small part of me remembered those days when Barbie went swimming in her super stylish late seventies bathing suit at Crestwood. Barbie was resilient. And I realized that the only thing that was ruined here was the box. Toys in their boxes are more valuable than not, and the only reason I cared about the box was the value it added because of the typo. But what was valuable to me was the doll inside. I did what every collector dreams of doing. I unboxed the Barbies.

It was going on two in the morning when I sat on the floor, surrounded by a small army of beauties. They'd been rinsed clean of any residual air conditioning leak, towel-dried as best as I could, and positioned on the doll stands that came with them. It was a moment of euphoria.

It was time to stop hiding that which I valued the most and start appreciating it. This is something we all need to learn. It was time to recognize that there were things that I had shoved in my own closet: talents, ideas, creativity, instincts, that I wanted to use more frequently. It was time to stop hiding the valuables and stick them out in the open where they became a part of my everyday life.

Now my army of Barbies sits on top of my dresser. Every once in awhile, but not too often, I buy a new one and unbox it. They remind me of the importance of appreciating what I have.

Glitter Matters

Glitter. Aside from being a bad Maria Carey movie, it's innocuous. Right? Wrong. Those tiny particles of reflective paper that get stuck in your hair, that get into the carpet fibers and onto your clothes, that linger months after the holiday where they were used to enhance a festive setting, those little buggers are unique.

Several years ago, aside from the craft stores where glitter is a basic item, you could buy it at trendy stores in the mall. But because of slow sales the store marked it down. From a discount shelf at the back of the store, a young woman bought a jar to sprinkle on her friends at a Fourth of July party on a beach.

How do I know all of this? Because of forensic science.

Here's a summary of events: Megan Barroso was at a beach party. Her friend sprinkled everyone with red glitter. On Megan's way home, someone shot her, then carried her body to a ravine and left her to die. Evidence gatherers found red glitter in Megan's hair.

There's a forensic scientist who specializes in glitter. He analyzed the sample and discovered it was red on one side, silver on the other–not like most glitter. It was octagonal in shape—also unusual. Because of the unique properties of the sample, he was able to trace it to Hot Topic, a store at the mall, where the red shade lived on the clearance shelves. Megan's friend verified that she had sprinkled people with the metallic pixie dust at the beach party. Why does this matter?

The police had a suspect. Tiny pieces of octagonal shaped glitter that was red on one side and silver on the other were found in his vehicle. And other than the red glitter, there was nothing to connect him with her murder.

But connect him, they did. Investigators connected the glitter from the friend's clearance-store purchase to the beach party to Megan's hair to the interior of the suspect's car to the ravine where Megan's body was found. And in doing so, the suspect became respectively the defendant, the convicted killer, and the inmate.

Like a piece of glitter stuck to my cheek, this story has gotten stuck in my head. I didn't know Megan Barroso. I have no connection with her other than watching an episode of *Forensic Files*. But as a mystery writer, I am fascinated with investigations, evidence, clues, and reality. And what strikes me about Megan Barroso's case is the reality. But glitter? As a clue to solve a murder? If it weren't so tragic, it would read like chick lit.

In life, as well as in fiction, the little things count.

The Jazz Made Me Cry

There are voices in my head, and I listen to them. At times they make me crazy because they won't give me a break. When I think there isn't room for another character, someone new elbows their way in and demands my attention. But the jazz made them all be quiet for one afternoon; the jazz gave me peace. Maybe that's why the jazz made me cry.

Before he passed away, Mike Melvoin, noted jazz pianist, performed an intimate concert in the back room of a piano store in Los Angeles. The Mike Melvoin trio was scheduled to kick off a series of Sunday afternoon jazz performances in the store and I was lucky enough to be one of the thirty or so people in the folding chairs taking it all in.

With a piano, bull fiddle, and drum kit, the trio provided audio Xanax, eliminating everything in my mind. The music engulfed me. Within minutes of the first song starting, tears trickled down my face. And if pressed to describe what I felt at that moment, it would have been simple. The jazz felt personal.

Aside from the concern that the bronzer I'd so carefully dusted on was now streaked, leaving a tiger-like make-up job on my face, and a mounting curiosity over where another audience member had purchased the mint-condition, white patent leather low-heeled boots that she tapped to the beat, I lost myself in the music. And after three songs, the army of amateur sleuths in my head were replaced with a virtual drill sergeant who told me to get it together. The performance was moving but I was sitting in the front row, after all.

For two hours, I was entranced. I closed my eyes and the rest of the world went away. Eighty-eight black and white keys peppered with the goosed up plucking of an upright bass and the rhythmic dusting of a drum kit and cymbals. I could have listened to it all afternoon.

The voices didn't go away for good, and I wouldn't want them to. In a lot of ways, they're what make me feel special. They pose questions that I answer, get into problems that I solve, and keep me inspired to write. But now I know, if the voices ever stop, I'll still have all that jazz.

If It Wasn't for All the Cat Hair

I could be a crazy cat lady if I wanted. All the instincts are there. I love cats, all cats, though the ones without the fur are a little weird. Not only do I see nothing wrong with someone owning upwards of, say ten, I think coming home to a house filled with little purring balls of fluff would be delightful.

I don't have any cats at the moment, so becoming a crazy cat lady would involve a bit of planning. I don't think I could get there overnight. I'd have to figure out what cat would be the first cat and go from there, because I think it would be important that Cat Number One not be a loner.

There would be supplies to buy: litterbox(es), food and water bowls, toys, carpet cleaner. There would be a change to my daily routine: feeding, litter changing, and lint rolling before I left each day. There is the slight matter of whether my landlord allows pets that creates a challenge. I could get a cat and keep it a secret, but to fully realize the goal of being a crazy cat lady, I'd need more than one cat, and it would be hard to hide this new way of life.

I would have to move.

My main goal has spiraled into several sub-goals, a checklist: find a place to live that will allow me to have a dozen cats. Give notice to my current apartment building. Pack up my belongings. Move. Unpack my belongings. Outfit the new apartment for a dozen cats. Buy a case of lint rollers. Find Cat Number One. Add in additional kitties from there.

See? It could be done. It wouldn't happen overnight, but it could be done if I wanted it badly enough.

There would be challenges along the way. My landlord might make me give two or three months notice instead of one. I might not find an apartment that allows a dozen cats, and if I did, they might require an extra deposit per cat. Deciding on Cat Number One, the one that's going to share my journey into crazy cat lady-dom with me and help nurture all of the other cats that come into the fold, might be harder than I think. I have to be prepared and adapt my plans accordingly.

Setting any goal is not unlike this process. We need to know the end goal. We need to keep the ball rolling and understand that some things take time. Different people's goals might be interchangeable, but the journey is the same. If we want the end result, we have to be prepared for bumps in the road.

Like any pursuit of goals, the labyrinth of the writer's path is fraught with roadblocks that sometimes seem like pee stains on a carpet, claw holes on the sofa, and cat yak on a favorite pair of shoes. But when you achieve your goal, it feels good.

Purring-cats-curled-up-on-your-bed good.

Why Do You Like Me?

Chances are, if you're reading this, then there's something about me or my writing that you like (or you think I'm your nemesis, in which case YOU HAVE TO TELL ME! Because I always thought it would be fun to have a nemesis, but you can't have one who wants to remain anonymous). Maybe we went to school together once. Maybe we worked together at some point or became friends along the way. Maybe we share writerly commiseration on a Yahoo group. Or maybe you're family.

No matter what the reason, you're here, and I'm here, so, like I said, I'm guessing you like me. What I'm curious about is why. Is it because I'm driven? Afraid of department store Santas? Sometimes rely on packing tape to secure the hem of my designer clothes?

Give me five minutes and I could rattle off a hundred likeable things about me, but that's not how it works, right? You don't like me because I told you to, or you found something about me that you related to, and that's what it's all about. That elusive connection.

A writer makes up people and makes up their lives, and aside from plot and description and dialogue and voice, has to figure out a way to make readers connect with the characters. The hard thing is, the connection between the writer and the characters is innate. The writer created these people. Trust me, if you're spending time writing 2,000 words a day about make-believe folks, you darn well better like them. But this means you have blinders on. Liking your characters is a natural for you, so imagine how it feels when someone else tells you they just didn't connect with them?

There's an exercise that's suggested to writers who are trying to expose their characters quirks and flaws: list twenty things that are unique about that character. Inevitably, you'll stall out before you hit ten, and you have to start thinking about details that shaped her (or him) that might never hit the page of your manuscript, but that help you figure out the kind of person she (or he) is.

Did she play the drums in high school, or the trombone, or sing in the chorus? Was she a cheerleader or did she try out five different times and never make the squad? Does she like Elvis? How much? So much that she'll sit in an uncomfortable theater seat all night for a King film festival? And when did she start liking Elvis? Did her parents take her to one of his concerts when she was a kid, or did she date an impersonator during college?

These details expose the character's character. Make this same list about yourself. Think about those little known facts that make you who you are that maybe nobody knows. Those facts shaped who you are and made you the person that other people respond to. The rest of the world doesn't need to know those facts to see the person you are.

That's how it is with writing. The more pressing question is this: how do you get this interesting and endearing information across on the page without an information dump?

Here's the thing. I love my characters. I spend enough time with these people that, in a weird way, they're like friends, only make-believe.

And because you like me, I want you to like my imaginary friends. It's only fair that we should all get along.

Goodbye Scooter

If you follow my status updates on Facebook, you know that my landlord demanded that I part with my college motor scooter. The demand had nothing to do with my college memories but more with the fact that it no longer ran and thus took up space in the parking garage. Not space where anyone else could park, mind you, but for some reason, having an inoperable cute red motor scooter occupying otherwise unusable space in the parking garage was not tolerable, and so, goodbye scooter.

I bought the scooter in 1986, my sophomore year at college. For three years I tooled around Williamsburg, jetting to classes, the caf, and anywhere else I could go without having to exceed thirty-five miles an hour. After I graduated, the scooter got me to swim team practice, my job, and a couple of other spots around Reading. When I moved away from my parents' house, the scooter stayed, occupying a corner of their garage.

Over the next ten years or so, the scooter went for a joyride once or twice a year, then reclaimed its spot in the garage. I moved to Texas. The scooter did not. Occasionally my dad asked if I was ready/willing to sell it. I wasn't.

Why not? It's not like I was using it. It's not like I even was looking at it. And I could have easily had the movers pack it up when they moved me to Texas. But I didn't.

Eventually, my parents drove south to visit me, with a van packed with all of the things from the attic, basement, and garage that they wanted to clear out. The scooter was in the mix. I happily parked it in my own garage, driving it around the block every once in awhile. There was something about the little William and Mary parking sticker on the back left side that pleased me. Kept me tethered to the person I was in college. Enough of my life had changed since I relied on it to get me around that I'd lost touch with who I had been in those days. The scooter had become my Rosebud.

Life changed again. I moved to California, changed jobs, started fresh. This time the movers packed the scooter. It worked when I left. It never worked after arriving. I hired people to fix it and was scammed out of fifty dollars. And after my landlord decreed that I had seven days to remove it from the parking garage, I had little choice. Yes, I could have loaned it to a friend. I could have rented a truck to transport it to a real scooter-repair business. I could have put it in storage. Or, I could acknowledge that the scooter had served its purpose, reminding me of who I once was during the days when I needed the reminder, and let it go.

So I did. I donated it to charity. The scooter can do something good for someone else now.

Goodbye, scooter.

Tarnishing My Image

People think I'm nice. I volunteer for a lot of projects, jump in to help out others when I have the time, and apologize for stuff that isn't my fault. All of this, I fear, is at odds with my desire to be taken seriously as a mystery writer. I mean, mystery writers are not nice people. They (we) think about crimes and dead people and motives. Sometimes blood and brain matter. Nice people don't sit around thinking about stuff like that, right?

So I think the next step in my ongoing attempt to become the mystery writer I want to be is to tarnish my image a bit. I came up with a couple of ideas:

1. Be mean to kittens and puppies. The fundamental issue with this is that my landlord won't allow me (or anyone) in my building to have a pet, despite the fact that I really, really want one. Which means that whenever I do see a cat or a dog, my voice rises a couple of notches like most people do around a baby, and I'm overcome with the desire to shower

it with love. So, option one, probably not going to happen.

2. Beat up a geek. See, I know about bullies, and their bad reputation. Does the name Scott Farkas ring any bells? And bullies don't pick on other bullies. They pick on geeks. The inherent problem with this option is that, on more than one occasion, I have participated in geeky behavior myself (two words: Comic-Con. Okay, that's one and a third words. But still, the fact that I did the math tells you something.)

3. Get arrested for something. Problem here is that I can't decide on a crime that I think would be okay to perpetrate. Maybe I could just ask a couple of cops to pretend arrest me? Because I don't want to do anything that will go on my permanent record.

4. Introduce a new signature expression. These days, when I'm exiting a conversation, I tend to say, "See ya!" or some version thereof. But maybe I'll replace "see ya" with "watch your back" I'll end every conversation like this.

> Examples:
> You: Have a good day!
> Me: Watch your back!
> —or—
> You: Be careful driving home.
> Me: Watch your back!
> —or—

You: Don't forget an umbrella.

Me: Yeah, watch your back!

That's it so far, but I'm open to suggestion. Just don't expect me to say thank you.

Use It or Lose It

I have these two stainless steel spoons that I bought at a sample sale at work. They don't match each other, but they were a quarter apiece, and the bowl of the spoons are very close to perfectly round, and since I'm inexplicably drawn to circles, I plunked down my fifty cents and made them mine. Most of the time I don't use them, because they don't match the other utensils in my drawer. And when I don't eat alone, I like all of the flatware to match. But one day I decided that these two mismatched sample sale bargains would be the designated ice cream spoons because I like ice cream, and this way they get to fulfill their spoon destiny.

Does that make me seem strange? (That is a rhetorical question.)

So, spoons and their destiny. Think about it. The entire purpose of these little round bowls on a stick is to transport food from our plates to our mouths. Not the kind of food that needs to be speared, because we use forks for that. If I never designated the ice cream usage, these two spoons would sit idle in my drawer forever. That saddens me.

As much as I like ice cream, I don't eat it all the time, which means the spoons often find themselves resting in the bottom of the utensil drawer under all of the other flatware that came from that nice, neat coordinating set I use for company. Then I got an inspired idea and added to their responsibilities. These are also the go-to spoons for stirring milk into coffee. And because I find myself sitting in front of a computer often, fingers not always ready to type the kind of clever prose you expect from me, I drink a lot of coffee.

I think that's nice. Not that I drink a lot of coffee, but that I have now added a second significant designated use to the mismatched spoons in the drawer. Though at the moment, I'm reminded that I have yet to have my first cup of coffee today, which might explain a thing or two.

I can't help thinking that life is a little bit more pleasing now that I can rely on the designated ice cream-slash-coffee spoons to get me through the day. They are always there when I need them. Some might even call them dependable.

We all have stuff that is not being used that has so much potential—stuff we can depend on when pressed. It's up to us to make better use of that which God, the universe, and/or Visa have provided to enrich our lives. If we don't use what we have, it's either going to perish or end up in a yard sale. And after it's gone, if we never used it to its full potential, we may never truly know what we missed.

It's like the Turkish coffee pot that I use to heat up olive oil to put on my popcorn. The vase that sat under my sink for ten years, until one day I put it on the counter and made it the paper towel holder. The Moon Boots I wear instead of slippers when my feet get cold. Or that weird dish where I toss my keys.

If you've got it, flaunt it. If you don't use it, you may lose it. We're surrounded by abundance. It's up to each of us to see it.

Pistachio

(SOMETIMES YOU FEEL LIKE A NUT)

It Ain't All Confetti

I once saw Rip Taylor perform a one-man show. (Go on, Google him. I'll wait.)

Yes, that Rip Taylor. Toupee, sequins, props, and more. I'd been expecting the toupee, sequins, and props. It was the "and more" that got me.

I didn't spend a lot of time reading about the show before attending because it was Rip Taylor, the man who made himself famous playing center square on the *Hollywood Squares*. Silly ostrich feather coats, confetti cannons, and "Happy Days Are Here Again."

When the producers announced, ahead of the show, that now would be a good time to use the restrooms because we were about to sit down for an hour and a half show, a shiver ran up my spine.

The show started with exactly what I anticipated. Rip took a bow and his toupee flipped down, revealing a patch of tape across his bald head. The jokes in the stack of rubberbanded cards were one-liners of the seventies game show variety. The props included lopsided bras, a six-pack of Coke taped to a cane, and a backdrop of sequined jackets.

And then the lights dimmed and Rip's narrative turned to stories of his childhood. He spoke of some not-very-nice stuff that happened to him. I was uncomfortable for a moment, thinking "This story should not end in a cheap joke." And it didn't.

I was completely engaged for the rest of the show as Mr. Taylor talked about the road he'd traveled, including both the lucky breaks and the unfortunate circumstances. He threw in punch lines when I wasn't expecting them which made me laugh out loud. He brought tears to my eyes, too.

Throughout the whole show, in the back of my mind, I thought to myself, "This is what editors mean by creating an emotional connection with your audience." Sure, Rip Taylor gave us humor, but it was blended with depth and truth and reality with a side order of fluff. That's the goal, at least for me: Make your audience laugh, but make them care, too. And after they care, make them laugh again. They'll care even more.

By the end of the show, when Rip Taylor shot rounds of brightly colored paper into the audience and proclaimed, "It ain't all confetti," I felt like I'd gotten way more than the price of admission.

That's Mine. Go Get Your Own.

I once saw an episode of *Antiques Roadshow* where a man was getting a pair of blue bottles appraised. His story of how he'd acquired them wasn't like the usual, "I found it at a flea market for a dollar" variety. In short, he'd gone to an auction with hopes of buying a shotgun. He overheard the auctioneer tell someone else that he was interested in a pair of blue bottles. Shotgun sat in the audience and waited until right before the bidding closed on the blue bottles and bid, winning the pair for $200. He said he keeps them in the box in a closet, except for every once in awhile when he pulled them out of the closet and showed people his "expensive blue jars."

This troubles me.

I love *Antiques Roadshow*. I watch it with fair regularity. I love watching people defend the items that their friends think are ugly. And then, when they find out that their one or two dollar purchase is worth thousands, well, it brings a tear to my eye. But Shotgun didn't do that. He didn't like the bottles. He didn't even enjoy his bottles.

He bought the bottles because someone else, someone in the know, wanted them first.

I found myself wanting the bottles to be worthless. Or wanting an unfortunate accident to occur, where the appraiser gestures widely and "accidentally" knocks one of the bottles to the floor, causing it to break into a thousand worthless bits of blue glass (you just know he was thinking about it, too).

Why does this trouble me so much? Because it reminds me that there are people who are willing to take what other people want. People who don't develop their own tastes and talents but are motivated by a different agenda. For them, success lies not in achieving their own goals, but in taking what someone else wants out from under them. And even more troubling is that this guy *did* go to the auction with a specific want in mind—he wanted to buy a shotgun—and he scrapped his own agenda in order to get what someone else wanted.

It's like if I went to a vintage clothing sale hoping to acquire a Pucci dress, and at the last minute spent my money on an early computer prototype instead because someone in line said she was interested in it. Yet, computers aren't my bag. Pucci is. See my point?

The blue bottles turned out to be late eighteenth century Chinese blue glass, valued at $4-6,000. And when the appraiser told the man what the pair was worth, guess what he said? "Yeah, it's a shotgun." Only, it's not.

Go after what you want. It'll mean more when you get it.

William Shatner Is a Con Man

On any given day you can turn on the TV and see William Shatner. Whether it's in a commercial or TV show, be it current or rerun, he exudes self-confidence. It is undeniable.

If, upon seeing his image you react to the literal: the tummy, the toupee, the plasticized expression in the eyes, and you find yourself questioning why you can't turn away, you soon write off whatever it was you were doing and watch because you accept the undeniable charisma that he possesses.

He is a confidence man of the highest degree, because he's built his career on having oodles of it. If our society elected a king, it just might be William Shatner.

Think about it. This man has had more lives than all of the Aristocats put together. He's been in some of the most highly regarded *Twilight Zone* episodes, several hit TV series, spokesperson for companies, and frequently cited as a "web sensation." He's done over two hundred acting projects and made at least as many appearances as himself since his career started in the early fifties.

I'm a big enough geek that I own the CD by William Shatner: "The Transformed Man." (Actually, it's a double CD. The other album is "The Two Sides Of Leonard Nimoy." I already admitted to being a geek). But don't even get me started on his "singing."

How does he do it? How has he continued to reinvent himself from Captain Kirk to TJ Hooker to The Big Giant Head to Denny Crane to Priceline ad-man? Why is his spoken word version of Rocket Man kind of like a sparkly luminous intersection at the heart of pop culture?

Because he's Shatner, and whatever he does, he does with confidence. It's as simple as that.

By being a caricature of himself, he has transcended being a caricature of himself. But that doesn't make sense, I hear you say. And it doesn't. Literally, it doesn't make sense. It's like M.C. Escher stairs that keep going up around the top of the building but you never quite figure out which side is the top of the building. OMG! Shatner's career is an optical illusion! Only it's not, because it's real.

In 2000, William Shatner was named the worst actor of the century by the Razzie awards. Five years later he garnered an Emmy and a Golden Globe. The man is an inspiration. At one point his career was so down that a special effects person painted a mask of his face white and used it in a horror movie.

That movie was *Halloween.*

But Shatner was such a punch line that a rubber mask of him

became the face of Mike Myers.

What's my point, you might ask? It's that we need to take a page from Shatner's book (metaphorically. I don't want a bunch of you running out and tearing pages from something he wrote. Yes! Shatner is a multi-published author!)

When we aren't happy, we shouldn't try to change ourselves, we should change our realities. If people think we can only do one thing, then do that one thing and do it well. And when they're least expecting it, set phasers to stun and do something else, too. If people think they know who we are and what we're capable of, we need to show them more. Give them the unexpected.

And. Occasionally. Talk. Like. This.

Shatner Redux

I saw William Shatner's one-man live show in Hollywood (because I'm that cool). My parents are Trekkies, so I have a solid comfort level with Klingons and green-skinned women. And, before I learned to ride a bike, I learned how to make the Vulcan hand salute (but I never mastered the nerve pinch, despite repeated attempts on my older sister).

But as much as I'd like to talk all about The Shat, I won't. Because this blog post isn't about him, it's about ~~me~~ indie authors everywhere. And authors who are watching the publishing industry from the sidelines, trying to figure out which way to go. Indie authors who aren't yet indie authors, but who are considering that path. And to them, I'll say what William Shatner said to ~~me~~ a room filled with patrons of his show: Don't be afraid of taking a risk.

I'm an indie author, but not because I jumped into the deep end of independent publishing early on. My first publishing credit was a short story in a traditionally published mystery anthology. Squarely on the fence of which-one-are-you? That was me. But not for long!

Don't be afraid of risks.

Before deciding to go indie, I spent a lot of time learning about the publishing industry. Like others, I honed my query letter, networked, took classes, and most importantly, I wrote. I did a lot of watching from the sidelines as the early pioneers of indie did their thing. And by the time I'd made my decision, I knew not only that I wanted to do it, but how I wanted to do it, too. So with a business background, a creative spirit, and a can-do attitude, I went about becoming an independently published author, set to publish my first mystery, *Designer Dirty Laundry*.

I started my own publishing imprint, Polyester Press. I hired a professional editor, bought ISBNs, arranged for my book to be available for preorder on Amazon and Barnes & Noble, printed ARCs for reviewers, wrote blurbs, and designed promotional material. I hired a publicist to plan my launch parties and met with a local bookstore owner to get feedback on every single thing I'd done (and find out what I'd maybe missed).

But as every author knows, it's not about having a book. It's about finding an audience for my book, and finding that audience has a thing or two to do with visibility. I volunteered for my local Sisters In Crime chapter. I contributed to more anthologies. I contacted reviewers and authors for quotes for the back cover, wrote guest blogs, and ran ARC giveaways on Goodreads. I set up preorders for my next book. I did for my career what I'd expected a publisher would do for my career because I became a publisher.

If an opportunity was missed, it was my fault, and that is one heck of a motivator.

Don't be afraid of risks. There will be people who tell you you're missing out on the publishing experience if you go indie, but I can tell you that you don't have to miss out on anything. Know what it is you want from your writing career and make it happen. It IS scary. It IS a lot of work. It does make ~~me~~ you do daily battle with ~~my~~ your overall scattered, seat-of-the-pants personality, forcing ~~me~~ you to focus on what has to get done. But it's all there, at ~~my~~ our fingertips. And it can, most definitely, lead to something unexpected.

Don't be afraid of risks. You have to explore these strange new worlds. Seek out new readers, new opportunities. You have to boldly go where—

You probably knew I was going to say that.

Eyebrows, Teeth, and Vulnerability

I'm currently obsessed with eyebrows.

I don't know when this happened. But lately, when I watch TV or a movie, I lose track of the plot in favor of studying the precise arch of the tweezed eyebrows on all of the women. I read an article once that said there are two immediate things a person can do to look younger: shape your brows and whiten your teeth.

Eyebrows. They're an odd thing to be obsessed with, but I often find myself thinking that I'm the only woman who does not know how to expertly draw on my brows. I never thought it would matter much, but when I see pictures of myself, where I appear to have no eyebrows, I figure something's got to give. And don't think I haven't tried to work it out; I end up looking like a drag queen.

And then there's white teeth. It doesn't take a rocket scientist to figure out why this one's true. Teeth, before they've been stained by vices like coffee and red wine, are white. Aside from the occasional cavity blamed on the Sugar Daddy addiction of my youth, my teeth were pretty white. Although, now that I think about it, they did receive a daily bleaching by chlorine. There are so many products and services out there to whiten one's teeth that it's mind boggling, but for the frugal person, swishing hydrogen peroxide around your mouth for one minute every night before bed will do the trick in about a week. Dollar store, people!

Now, eyebrows make me think of Brooke Shields and Liz Taylor, but white teeth make me think of Donny Osmond. (Stay with me. I've got a point.) When Donny Osmond was on *Dancing with the Stars*, he clowned around. But when they showed the footage of him training to do the rumba, I was struck by something. Donny was concerned. He knew pulling off a serious rumba was going to be a challenge, and he put aside his goofball shtick to listen to his partner and learn the dance. He made mistakes in practice, and he knew it. And instead of laughing it off into a joke for viewer votes, he tried harder. He let down his guard. He wasn't smiling at the time, so his trademark smile wasn't on display, but in a flash of vulnerability, he looked like a younger version of himself.

That's when it hit me. When we let down our guards, when we let people see our flaws, that's when people are drawn to us. We show the world a flash of the person we once were, before life with a capital *L* kicked us to the curb. Before we toughened up so we could deal with stuff with a capital *S*.

That's when we are most real.

Perfection has a place, but truly interesting characters aren't perfect. You might be mesmerized by the well-dressed, graceful, white-toothed people of the world. But without discovering if they have a story behind their image, they might as well be life-sized cardboard cutouts. It is our imperfections that make us vulnerable and keep us interesting. It's the people that interrupt their image by occasionally slipping on a banana peel or exposing their undies in public that we want to get to know.

Because They're Green and Squishy, That's Why!

"**H**i, I'm Diane. I've heard good things about you. It's nice to finally meet."

I'm not talking about *you*. I'm talking about this avocado in front of me.

This oddly green and decidedly tasty fruity-vegetabley-fruit. (It's a fruit. But a vegetable-y one at that, which makes it a little suspect.)

A credible source says you could live for a year on dark chocolate, avocadoes, and mayonnaise. I say, sign me up! Because now that I know mayo is just olive oil and eggs, I'm pretty sure if trapped on a desert island, I could fry up some leaves when I needed a snack.

But my point is, I didn't know I liked avocadoes. I thought they looked weird, like green mashed potatoes wrapped up in a textured casing that looks like a grenade that was waterlogged then left out in the sun too long. I always said no thanks when they were offered to me.

Avocados never made me think too hard about weapons of mass destruction, but they did make me think about lasagna. Apparently I didn't like that either, until one day I read an article in the newspaper that said it was Donny Osmond's favorite food. (It was 1976 or so. Donny Osmond made quite the impression on me that year.) My parents found it odd that suddenly my older sister and I were asking for the same meal we'd made faces at and pretended to choke down. Surprisingly, lasagna remains one of the dishes I can make without a recipe. (Ish. I sometimes have to check the cheese-to-sauce ratio.)

It's a good thing I grew up with a polish grandmother, because things like halupkies became part of my life before I realized the word was strange. And if you had told me you were going to wrap up some meat and rice in a cabbage leaf and cook it for a zillion hours, I don't think we'd be sitting down together for dinner that night. But I can vouch for the fact that halupkies are YUMMY!

You see where I'm going with this, right? You gotta learn to try something new every now and then. Sometimes things look weird, and sometimes they sound weird, but if you give them a chance, you might like them. Maybe you think you don't like scary movies. And then the next thing you know, Hitchcock is your favorite director, and you've got *Psycho* on repeat. Maybe you've spent most of your life fighting your naturally curly hair and then one day you let it air dry and realize it's actually kinda cool. Maybe you think you're afraid of rejection, then you ask for criticism and discover you can end up with a better version of whatever you were trying to do.

Or maybe that's just me.

Is Liking Cats a Waste of Time?

The other day I was scrolling through my Facebook newsfeed, liking various posts from friends. Being a cat person without a cat, when I see a cute feline photo, I click the like button. That day was cat-heavy, and I was liking up a storm. The next thing you know . . . twenty minutes had gone by! TWENTY MINUTES. I'd lost a third of an hour because I was liking cats.

Time has become a precious commodity. Everybody I know is busy: with kids, with activities, with hobbies, second jobs, volunteer commitments. I'm no exception. Twenty minutes is no small chunk of change in the wallet of the ticking clock, and now I've got timetables to adhere to and deadlines to meet.

I keep detailed to-do lists and break my deadlines down into smaller deadlines that go onto my calendar—in pen. I limit myself to checking sales figures twice a day, and I've all but stopped typing my name into search engines. But as hard as I try to come up with pockets of time where I can become more productive, I wonder, is this everyone's problem? Are we all so busy that the frittering away of time—on Facebook, Twitter, Instagram, Goodreads, LinkedIn, Pinterest—has become a necessary escape that allows our brains to recharge?

Sometimes it feels like social media is stealing our lives from us in five-minute intervals. It can make us feel inadequate by comparison to the success stories that fill our feeds, and it can drain us with political opinions and unanticipated criticism.

But if you curate your newsfeed, surrounding yourself with supportive friends and positive vibes, it can become the five-minute break between sets of life that allows us to keep on keeping on.

Besides, I'm pretty sure cat videos will ultimately lead to world peace.

A Chance of Showers

I don't like to shower. I do it every single day, but I don't like it. It takes up time, but it does make me acknowledge my general appreciation for the world at large. There's the shampooing and the conditioning and the washing. After the shower, there's the getting ready, the I-can't-leave-my-hair-in-a-towel-turban-all-day part (which would be so much easier), the picking-out-an-outfit part, the do-I-or-don't-I-need-Spanx-under-this-ensemble part.

When I have a day off, there's something so freeing about getting up, pony-tailing my hair, and going directly to the computer to write. More than one joke has been made about writers who stay in their pajamas all day, and I can't say that the jokes are entirely off base. My computer doesn't take offense when I don't shower until the afternoon (I don't think), although it occasionally mocks me by not saving a document or blowing up a flash drive, so maybe it's just passive-aggressive.

There's a guilty pleasure in getting up and going directly to writing-work, something that says that the writing part of my day is so important, or so much fun, that when I have the time, it is the number one thing I want to do. My mind, when I first wake up, is already "clean." As in, not distracted by the internet, the news, the weather, the almost-car accident out front, or the fact that the grocery store is out of Neapolitan ice cream again. Starting my day by sitting down and typing says, "That shower can come later, before you head out into the world and get all angered by the crazy drivers. But right now, this is time for YOU."

Nobody knows this is my routine (okay, a few people know. The cable repair guy knew last week, and I'm sure my neighbor across the courtyard is suspicious) but all in all, it doesn't matter to anybody.

Aside from making me all shiny and clean, a shower says, "I'm ready to face the world." But sitting my butt in the chair, with my fingers on the keys, says, "I'm ready to tackle my personal goals." There's something empowering in that notion. By the afternoon, when I venture out, I feel better because of the work I've already done when my mind was clear, before I got into a fight with the mailman. And, I guess, if I took to showering at the end of the day, too, it would be my way of saying, "Hey world, you threw some real crap at me today, and look! It all washes off!"

But that would mean I'd be showering twice a day, and nobody has that kind of time.

Luck

When I was in junior high school, I tried out for the cheerleading squad. And let me tell you, I really, really, really wanted to make it. To this day I don't know why it was so important: the camaraderie? The outfits? The perceived popularity that went with being on the squad? What I do know is that my friends and I practiced our cheers every chance we got before those auditions.

On the day the team was posted, my dreams of flailing pompoms in a choreographed dance routine were dashed. I didn't make the squad. Later that afternoon, our principal called an assembly of every girl who had tried out. The judges had been so impressed with the talent that they had decided to add three additional spots to the team.

I didn't get one of the additional spots. My friend did. And I remember chowing down on a big bunch of sour grapes and thinking, clearly the only reason she made it and I didn't was luck.

It couldn't have been that I'm a natural klutz and maybe didn't have the best audition in the world.

It couldn't have been that I can't jump more than six inches off the ground.

It couldn't have been that I had other after school commitments and wouldn't have been able to keep up with the rehearsal schedule.

It couldn't have been that she was better than I was.

It was easier to blame the outcome on either her luck or my lack thereof. But in a pretty solid way, that was an insult to both of us. If luck had truly been a factor, then everything else must have been equal: our splits, our cartwheels, our handstands, our coordination. And how possible is it that our auditions went down the exact same way?

Not very. Because I still remember how my audition went, and while I may have the personality for it, my performance would have led to a public shaming.

Artisan
(FOR YOUR CREATIVE PASSIONS)

Life Is a Musical

I have a serrated kitchen knife that gets regular use for one reason. Its knife destiny was intended to slice bread, but I've found it to be the perfect knife to use to dice tomatoes. Whenever tomatoes need to be sliced and/or diced, I open the knife drawer and get out the tomato knife. And, it takes about three seconds from me putting my hands on the tomato knife to me singing the tomato knife song, which is to be sung to the tune of Beethoven's 5th Symphony: "To-Ma-To Knife. To-Ma-To-Knife. To-Ma-To Knife, Knife KNIIIIIIIIIIFE! TOE-MAY-TOE-knife . . ." and quickly morphs into "Bohemian Rhapsody" (I'm not sure why), and then the rocking out starts.

I admit, busting out into the Tomato Knife Song is slightly less theatrical than performing a choreographed song and dance routine (I've yet to add moves to the Tomato Knife Song, which is probably wise since I'd be doing said moves with a knife in my hand) but it is what it is: a spontaneous celebration of something mundane. And I enjoy the process of slicing tomatoes so much more now that the process has its own musical number. Which leads me to the point of this blog: life as a musical.

Sometimes music breaks the monotony of life. Who among us doesn't feel better after singing along to "Greased Lightning?" And the *Grease 2* song about reproduction should be part of every high school curriculum.

Let's leave Rydell High for a moment. What about "So Long, Farewell" from *The Sound of Music?* It's a song about saying good night.

Advertising companies learned long ago that catchy tunes + products = winning formula. Musicians learned it, too, when advertising companies came knocking on their doors for the rights to their songs. Are you telling me you don't remember the "Stuck in the Middle With Me" commercials for Hanes Her Way panties?

Life isn't easy. We encounter people who make us angry, obstacles that keep us from achieving our goals, and ever-shifting timetables that force us to reassess where we are in life. In order to get through the day we have to accept the realities of showering, laundry, cleaning the dishes, and pumping gas. Why not turn your entire life into a musical to get you through it?

Six A.M. Is a State of Mind

While California is generally sunny and seventy-five degrees, there's this thing that happens every June, this dingy white-ness that makes the sky look like dirty tile on a shower stall and makes everything else gray around the edges, like the whole city just went on a bender. It's known as June Gloom, and it's more than a visual dulling down of Los Angeles. It's a state of mind.

I didn't notice June Gloom right away. It took a few weeks to realize that my mood was down and that my natural energy reserves were tapped and seemingly non-renewable. My mental acuity would go on the fritz and my motivation was, if not out the window, cowering under the covers not wanting to get out of bed.

Being a creative person, this lack of ignition is alarming. Why didn't I have any ideas? Why didn't I want to write? What happened to my passion? Was it gone? Would it come back?

Concerning questions, I thought.

Drastic measures needed, I decided to hit the gloom head-on. Shock it out of my system, so to speak. I dragged myself out of bed at 6 a.m. (and no morning person am I) and drove to the beach. It was cool and overcast, but I was prepared. Blanket to lie on, blanket to cover with. Pillow. Book. Free parking until nine o'clock, and nothing but the sound of waves crashing to distract me. By the time the afternoon rolled around, I was in a perky mood, already feeling better.

I kept up the system-shocking regimen. Early morning walks. Early morning swims. Earl morning visits to the flower market.

(Who knew there was so much to do before 7 a.m.?)

What I've discovered is it's not so much what I'm doing that shakes me out of a stagnant mental state, but the fact that I'm making myself do it. If you told me a month ago that I'd willingly get up at six to do just about anything I'd tell you that you had the wrong girl. And when California turns green in July and the bursting blue sky and bright sun combo make sleeping in impossible, I'll probably forget my troubles and get happy. You find what works and you do it, even if it's opposite every impulse you have.

Now, if you'll excuse me, it's time for my nap.

It Started with a Gallon of Yellow Paint

A couple of months ago I got the itch to paint my dining room yellow (the probable result of Doris Day overexposure). I also wanted to spruce up the office, which is next to the dining room, but I didn't want a yellow office. I wanted an aqua office. And as long as I'm talking about what I wanted, I wanted a round doorway like the kind you believe are very common if you watch a lot of movies from the sixties.

Adaptable me came up with an inspired solution. I stenciled a seven-foot diameter circle around my front door and painted the interior of the circle white. I painted the dining room yellow, defining the left side of the circle. I painted the office aqua, defining the right side of the circle.

Yes, it was a silly room.

As it happens, these three areas: the dining room, front door, and office frame out the Career and Life Plan area of my apartment. (If this is at all interesting to you, I highly recommend Karen Rauch

Carter's book *Move Your Stuff, Change Your Life*.) As I painted, I realized that I've paid little attention to this area and half-wondered if I would notice a difference thanks to the decorating effort. (I am a skeptical believer in Feng Shui.)

I didn't gain an unexpected promotion. I didn't fall into a cushy job or get rewarded with accolades at the job I held. What I gained was more valuable than any of those. I gained a clear picture of what I wanted.

Four years ago, I decided I wanted to "be a writer". I'd been writing before coming to that conclusion, but my decision meant I wanted to take it seriously. I changed up my whole life and pursued the path the way I knew how: query agents, edit, rewrite, polish, enter contests, take classes. During the past four years I watched the upheaval of the publishing industry while almost tripling my number of completed manuscripts. I felt like I was in a car stuck in the mud, tires spinning. My foot was pressed on the gas pedal, even though I was getting nowhere, because it was the only way I'd been taught to drive.

After I finished painting the aforementioned rooms, I looked into self-publishing. The more I researched, the more excited I felt. I didn't go to bed until well past midnight because I was wide awake, devouring knowledge about formatting, marketing, templates, and time tables. Not one to make a rash decision (textbook Capricorn) I kept my thoughts mostly to myself until I was comfortable with my decision.

I got comfortable.

Who knew yellow and aqua were the colors of clarity?

Critical Mass

I have a friend who has sworn off movies that get a D rating. I have no such rule, as can be noted by my choice of movies to see in a theater: *Burlesque? Ocean's Thirteen? Sex and the City 2?*

The thing about movies that get bad reviews is that they were made by people who cared enough to make them. Somebody believed in the movie, otherwise, more people would be at home reading on a Friday night (hmm . . .).

So what if these movies got a bad review? The directors did something. They created something. They stood for something. Seeing the criticism pile up against them is good for one thing: reminding us that if we try to do something, there will be criticism. Period.

Think about how awful it is, to go ahead with a project knowing that there will be criticism.

Now think about how empowering it is to go ahead with a

project knowing that there will be criticism.

That's right, I said empowering. Why? Because while you can control the quality of your project, the content of your project, the packaging for your project, and the promotion of your project, you can't control the criticism of your project. Accept it and move on.

One of my favorite inspirational movies is *Unzipped*, the fashion documentary from 1995. The movie follows Isaac Mizrahi as he conceptualizes his collection and mounts his runway show. You see how much goes into that collection: living it, breathing it, searching for signs and inspirations that he's on the right track; then the frustration of recognizing when someone else channels the same muse as him, and the mounting stress of getting it all done. And then, when it's done, watching him acknowledge that regardless of what people said, it's about taking the next step toward a new project.

The movie says so much about Mizrahi's mettle and serves as a guide to the kind of creative mettle I want to have. His actions say "Follow my example. Know when to ask for help, but know what you want to stand for."

So, kudos to those who take a chance and go ahead with their visions. Kudos to the makers of poorly received movies (and the makers of well received movies, because we shouldn't hold their five stars against them), for setting the example for the rest of us that it's more important to try something than to be afraid to try for fear of what people will say. Because even if it's inevitable that there will be criticism, there's always the chance that there will be praise, too.

Stupid is as Stupid Does

I had a math teacher in eighth grade who charged his students a ten cent fine for making a stupid mistake on a test. Things like adding four + three and getting twelve. Forgetting to carry the one. Solving an equation for X instead of Y. Ethical or not, a year's worth of ten cent errors from the class bought us a pizza party in the spring. From this, I learned two important lessons:

1. Stupid mistakes will cost you, and
2. If you make enough stupid mistakes, you get pizza.

For the purposes of this blog, I'll focus on point one.

I recently made a stupid mistake. On a scale of one to ten, I call it a humdinger (which isn't actually on a scale of one to ten so you can start to see how big it was). I hired a freelance editor to give me feedback on a to-be-published manuscript, and I sent her the wrong file.

I sent her the wrong file.

And I didn't discover my mistake until she finished the job and sent the completed edit back to me.

This mistake wasted my money and another person's time. It created a spiral of self-doubt and a cycle of self-inflicted head slapping and kicking. There may have been a firm talking to from myself to me. It's kind of a blur.

I remind myself that this isn't the first time I've done something stupid, and it won't be the last. Not surprisingly, that speech doesn't help. I tell myself that people do stupid things all the time. Not knowing the details of other people's stupid mistakes does little to assuage my feelings of self criticism and does even less to help me believe this is the last time I will do it.

What gets me, more than the stupid mistake, is the energy expended in beating myself up afterward. What caused this kind of error? Self-sabotage? Carelessness? Fear of failure? A good Sauvignon Blanc?

The fact of the matter is that we all DO do it, but some of us recover faster than others. Maybe that's the true test. It's not whether you win or lose. It's not how you play the game either. It's what you do when you trip and fall and discover that you left your shoes tied together before you started the race that counts.

If I leave my shoes tied together before starting a race, I hope I'll have the sense to stop, untie them, and get on with it instead of falling down and staying down. Because as we all know, stopping mid-race doesn't get us anything, whereas finishing can get us two things:

1. A huge sense of accomplishment, and
2. Pizza.

Moon Mission

Last night I was watching a documentary on the moon mission. Watching the footage of these men who were blasted off into outer space, who were going into unfamiliar territory, who were pioneers in their own right, was inspirational.

Most people can come close to reciting Neil Armstrong's words upon setting foot on the moon's surface, "That's one small step for man, one giant leap for mankind," but aren't even aware of Buzz Aldrin's statement after following Armstrong to the moon's surface: "That might have been a small step for Neil, but it was a big step for me."

In my mind, while Armstrong's words are profound, Aldrin's are honest. There is a humility in them, an awe over what he has just accomplished. And despite the grandeur of Aldrin being on the moon and the rest of the world watching or listening to the event, we know how he feels.

When you dabble in the word trade, it's easy to obsess over every sentence, every plot point. It's also easy to stop writing because of the fear of where you're going. It's easy to be intimidated by what others have accomplished that you have not, because you never know if you're going to get there, too. But when you reach the milestones: writing a first sentence, finishing a first draft, getting feedback from a first reader, sending out first queries, receiving the first request for material, reading that first acceptance of your work from a publisher. The occasions are no less momentous because someone else has done them first.

Writers are pioneers of the page, discovering our story as we type or handwrite the words. We'll make false starts and have aborted missions. But if we allow ourselves to move into that unknown territory of plot, character, and voice, we'll discover things along the way. And no matter how many drafts we write, when we finish one, it is a big step. It's cause for celebration!

Neil Armstrong has admitted that he flubbed his line upon landing on the moon, proving that everyone wants a chance to go back and self-edit. But that's a whole different subject!

Dreams

Back when I first discovered how much I wanted to write, I worked a full time job and had to fit my manuscript into weekend mornings and transatlantic flights. The more I wrote, the more I wanted to write, and I became increasingly aware of the fact that my lifestyle required me to pursue the job, not the dream. I don't even know if I saw writing as a dream at that point. I only remember how alive I felt when I was sitting at a desk making up stories, versus the rest of my life where I went through the motions.

Writing was an escape. It pulled me out of a time in my life when I wasn't happy. It distracted me from the time I spent traveling for work. It gave me a sense of confidence that I hadn't discovered even though I'd experienced a small amount of professional success.

There were those who saw it as a hobby. Those who saw it as a waste of time. Those who criticized me. But there were also those who asked to read what I'd written. Who encouraged me to keep going. Who allowed me to believe that it was okay to spend my time doing something that felt so right. And because of these people, I allowed myself to fantasize about being a writer.

That right there is the key. It's about letting a part of yourself imagine what it would be like to be the name on the books in the bookstore. To see a stranger reading your book in a coffee shop. To be acknowledged for the characters you create. The dream isn't about seeing yourself at a keyboard staring at a blank screen. It's about the moments beyond that, when you've broken through those daily struggles to get words on the page.

The dream is a bigger picture. Like a coffee shop hostess who imagines herself accepting the Academy Award. The dream is usually light years from where we are, but it's necessary to have that fantasy in order to move in that direction.

Is it worth indulging in the fantasy of wild success? Absolutely. Because without our active imaginations, we're not equipped to do the one thing we want to do. Even if you keep it to yourself, go ahead and let yourself dream. You deserve it.

Detective and Buyer: More Alike Than You'd Think

An interesting thing occurred to me while attending Homicide School. That is, the similarity in skill sets between a detective and a retail buyer. You have two very different jobs that have two very different intentions and outcomes (also very different wardrobes. Refer to a fashion buyer's outfit as plain clothes? Never!) but consider a couple of similarities:

1. An ability to look at a large assortment of data and edit it down into something meaningful. A detective will arrive at the scene of a crime and be faced with the results of what happened. It is her job to assess what she's looking at and determine which parts of it relate to the crime. A buyer will arrive at a designer's showroom and be faced with a collection of samples. It is her job to assess what she's looking at and determine which parts of it relate to her store's target customer base.

2. A balance between creative and analytical thinking. A detective needs to intuitively recognize angles when determining gunshot trajectory and direction of blood spatter. She also needs to create a variety of "what happened here" theories until one fits. A retail buyer needs to recognize salability in a product based on sales history. She also needs to create a cohesive assortment and take risks on something different in order to stay ahead of the curve.

3. Relying on a strong gut feeling. A detective needs to run high on intuition, a sense of "something isn't right" here. A quick theory might be based on this intuition, but when several detectives have the same gut feeling it often points an investigation in the right direction. A buyer needs to run high on intuition, too, looking at sometimes a hundred samples and zeroing in on the ten that stand out. A buyer for a large organization might have the opportunity to hear co-workers' gut feelings, too, which make for a better assortment overall.

4. Flourishes with a flexible workload. Most detectives are happier in the field than at a desk but don't always know the direction their day will take them. Most retail buyers successfully juggle a balance of showroom appointments, travel, order writing, projections, recaps, and store interaction.

5. Gets results. Sure, the end results of these two jobs are vastly different, but they are both result-oriented.

6. Both enjoy a breakfast of donuts and coffee.

One of the series that I write runs off the assumption that a former retail buyer, suspected of murder, can expose the real killer in order to prove her innocence. She doesn't exactly go about it in a neat, normal way, but like a detective, she gets results.

Postscript: Would you rather have a retail buyer solve a crime, or a homicide detective determine next season's trends?

Life Imitating Art Imitating the Road Not Taken

It was 1987, but I remember it as though it was yesterday. I was a poor college student. Poor, because my parents determined that $70 was enough to cover my monthly expenses, I lived in an apartment off campus with three other girls and tried to live on a budget. Misinformed retailers put me on their mailing list. That's how I first saw the boots. They were three colored, zip apart perfection, and they were $220.

At first that two-hundred and twenty dollars was waaaaaay beyond my means, even for zip apart perfection. But, because I was currently enrolled in an Economics course (that taught me about projections and other budgetary calculations that you think you're never going to use in real life but it turns out you use all the time when you want to buy something new) I broke that $220 down into $2/day for the next 110 days. To the young, optimistic, world-is-my-oyster student that I was, zip-apart perfection seemed within my reach. The school year had barely started; I could own the boots by Thanksgiving!

I started with the best of intentions. Every night I tucked $2 into a crisp white envelope that sat next to my bed. One week later, having made numerous financial sacrifices and digging all of the change out of the bottom of the hamper, I was on track. The envelope was smudged, crinkled, and held $14.

Fourteen dollars is not enough to buy fantastic, awe-inspiring zip apart boots. Fourteen dollars, at that time, barely bought a week's worth of eggroll dinners. Slowly, painfully, I let the thought of those boots slip away from the land of possibilities.

Fast-forward to a few years shy of today. I had decided to write a book. When I started writing the first draft, I knew my main character pretty well. Samantha Kidd might not have been dealt a normal-size portion of common sense, but she had moxie. She had guts. She was a lot of things that I was and a lot of things that I wasn't, and she found herself in a lot of situations that I wouldn't begin to know how to deal with.

But most of all, when she found herself indulging in escapist shopping therapy (When the going gets tough, the tough go shopping. That's what my mom taught me) she had the money to buy—you guessed it—a great pair of boots. THE boots. I remembered them with the kind of longing usually reserved for a past love, so I wrote them into a discount shoe outlet where they happened to be sitting on a markdown rack in Samantha's size. It was a sign that everything was going to be all right. Or, it was a sign that her priorities were severely out of whack. Either way she plunked down her credit card and bought the boots. (It's my book. If I want to deal with the ghosts of footwear past, I can.)

It was my way of getting reacquainted with the road less traveled. The "what-would-my-life-be-like-if-only-I'd-bought-those-boots" parallel universe. (I'm big on the road not traveled.)

Fast forward to the most satisfying long-term relationship I've had that started on the internet: eBay (Those eHarmony people are right when they say that true love can be found on the internet. I've got the miscellaneous but completely satisfying resold treasures to prove it). One evening I checked in and discovered, to my surprise and delight, a list tailor-made for me: "Items we think you'll like" (My dear eBay! You know me so well!). Smack, dab, at the forefront of the list were the boots.

Did you read that correctly? I said, The Boots. Capital *T*, capital *B*.

In. My. Size.

The *Twilight Zone* music playing in my head distracted me from buying them that night, and quite possibly the fear of getting what I wanted and being let down by reality kept me from clicking the Buy It Now button for the next few weeks (I admit to a few ill-conceived purchases along the way). Either that or I'm just a lazy procrastinator willing to tempt fate and the internet. But one day, Fate whispered a sweet nothing at me that I couldn't ignore. The boots were 45 percent off.

Buy It Now.

CLICK!

It took twenty-two years after discovering the boots for me to own them. That makes me love them all the more. And whenever I look at said boots, I think about my past. I think about my future. I think about timing, and how some things are meant to be.

But most of all, I think about the fact that I'm now wandering along the road not taken so many years ago. I'm ready for the future. And in these boots, I feel invincible.

Make It Work

Any designer who's faced a *Project Runway* challenge with a misfiring vision knows, often times genius involves a "make it work" moment. Tim Gunn didn't just coin a catch-phrase when he first said that, he put a new spin on suck it up, deal with it, and the more verbose "if at first you don't succeed, try, try again." If you like *Project Runway*, you love those moments. If you don't, chances are you've still hit that dead end somewhere along the way and had to either abandon what you're trying to do or figure out a new way to get to where you're going.

I don't think it matters how well you plan your journey, or to what extent you manage the steps to completing your goal. You can make lists. You can set timetables. You can have monthly goals, weekly goals, daily goals, or hourly goals. The ability to plan isn't the success factor because, somewhere along the way, you're going to hit an obstruction. And at that moment, it's less about what you anticipated and more about how well you roll with the unexpected punches.

Take, for example director Peter Bogdanovich. For his first directorial opportunity, he was given a unique challenge: studio head Roger Corman told him he could make any film he wanted, provided he

1. used Boris Karloff, who owed the studio two days work,
2. used footage from Karloff's recent movie *The Terror*, and
3. stayed under budget.

The Terror, part of the Poe-esque horror movie genre, was a far cry from the new wave director's vision. But challenges are often inspiring, and Bogdanovich made it work. He wrote and directed *Targets*, a thriller, which launched his career. He could have made a horror movie like so many others in the Karloff canon, but he pushed himself instead. If he'd played it safe, he might never have had the opportunity to make his second movie, *The Last Picture Show*.

We all face "make it work" moments. They might be getting un-stumped from a manuscript that stalls about half-way or throwing an impromptu dinner party when all you have on hand are celery sticks, beef jerky, and ramen noodles. They might be an opportunity to get where you want to be, but with all of the known roads closed for construction.

If you really want to succeed, you make it work.

It's Like Steak When It's Resting

Have you heard this? That after a steak comes off the flame or out of the oven, it needs to rest for a couple of minutes before it's at its yummiest and is ready to eat. Weird, right?

Although I've learned a thing or two about the kind of magic that happens in the kitchen, I'm not too proud to admit that my cooking life is underdeveloped. Before ten years ago, I'd never made mashed potatoes that didn't come from a box with the word *flakes* on the front. (But "potato flakes"? Pretty cool concept. It's like snow imported from Idaho.)

When a culinary artist offered to make steak Diane for me one night, (Oh, come on. You would eat a meal named after you, too) I was super excited, because my steak-making experiences had always left me with a hockey puck-textured piece of meat no matter how much meat tenderizer I used. But on this night, the steaks came out of the oven, onto a plate, were topped with a piece of tinfoil, and attention was turned toward the making of the side dishes.

Bad timing, I thought, although I was not one to question the culinary artist, so I kept my mouth shut. But a part of me wondered why he hadn't anticipated the steaks being done before the rest of the food and if my highly anticipated Steak Diane was going to have to be microwaved (say it ain't so!). All sorts of doubts about dinner infiltrated my mind while he whipped potatoes (or sliced and diced them–I can't remember. There were potatoes, and they didn't come from a box), flash fried asparagus, and made a mess in the kitchen (I'd be the one to clean it up—the price you pay for being the onlooker of dinner).

To my surprise, the intent was to let the steaks sit by themselves. No, they hadn't been bad, relegated to the corner in dunce hats, but apparently there's this thing that steaks do when they come out of the heat. Their juices run out, but if you give them a second, they reverse the process and reclaim them. And after that's done, they're better than if you didn't wait for them to do their thing.

That's some freaky s**t right there.

My instincts would have been to plop those steaks on the plates the second they came out of the oven, drizzle the juices on top of them, and sop up the juices that ran out when I cut into it. My instincts would have been to eat the steak before it was ready.

This is how I feel after I've finished a first draft. On more than one occasion I've been writing a manuscript and mention (to those close enough to me to hear this kind of modest self-aware observation), "This is pure gold, I tell you! Pure gold!" When the story is finished, my instincts are to write up a blurb and a query letter, look up the appropriate agents, and fire that bad boy off into the email ether because I want to share my pure gold with the world.

Unfortunately, I've learned that as valuable as pure gold is, it stands out even more when someone takes the time to shine it up a little bit. It has to be back-burnered, slightly forgotten, so it can be chewed, savored, seasoned, polished, and viewed with a critical eye toward making it even more enjoyable. It's like steak. So, like steak, my recent manuscript is resting, soaking up its juices, waiting for me to come back at it and make it even better.

I'm still not sure if the tin foil hat makes a difference.

In the Driver's Seat

I was recently involved in a car accident. I had been on my way home from work. Traffic was heavy, and a car hit me from behind. Most of us have been in accidents at some time in our lives, so you know what happened next: exchange info, take car to garage, get rental, deal with insurance companies. That's all pretty standard. And as far as things go, it was a textbook accident. Claims were filed; cars were repaired. Life went on.

So why am I talking about it now?

I was more shaken up by it than I thought I'd be. One minute I was fine, the next minute I wasn't. Through no fault of my own, things changed like *that* (insert finger snap here). And after dealing with the business end of the transaction (which had the odd side effect of calming me down by focusing on details like license plate numbers and personal contact info), it dawned on me that I was lucky. Not to be hit by a car, but that it was what it was and not something worse.

Thanks to the accident, I find myself thinking differently about a lot of things. I don't assume that tomorrow will be like today, because maybe it won't. And I recognize that I have a certain power in that today-tomorrow-the-next-day expectation, because I can expect it all to be the same (relinquishing power to change it) or forcibly make it different (by making different choices).

Thanks to the accident, I find myself looking backward in addition to looking forward. Literally, I am aware of the drivers in my rear view mirror, willing them to stop with a decent cushion of space between our bumpers, but also aware of the drivers in front of me, making sure that I leave that same cushion of space.

Figuratively, I am aware of what I've accomplished. I moved from Texas to California to pursue creative and personal goals set by me versus corporate ones set by others. Like the literal impact of the accident, I'm looking behind me, to my accomplishments, but also looking ahead to see how I can take even more ownership of my future.

Standing still is safe and painless. Moving forward can, on occasion, cause you a pain in the neck. But maybe it's worth it, if only to serve as a reminder of how far you've come when you look in your rear view mirror.

From Diane:

Twelve years ago, I chose to give up the way of life I knew and pursue passion-based goals. Moving to an unfamiliar state provided a metaphorical clean slate. Had I known then what I know now, what else would I have do ne differently?

Twelve years is long enough for other things. Relationships end. Lessons are learned. Doors are closed. Others are opened.

You might think I have a laundry list of decisions I'd change, but I don't. I spent it regaining my sense of self after realizing I was on the wrong path in my life in more than one way. I established new priorities, made a couple of sacrifices, and bought Pucci dresses. I wrote a lot, too.

In those years, I learned that not only could I write more than one book, I could write more than one series and more than one genre. I learned that some people liked what I wrote, and others didn't. I discovered a community of people who were trying to do exactly what I was, but instead of competing, they worked together. I joined them. The connections I made during that time are a reminder that life is not what we leave behind. There is never a day when we have to say, "I'm done." Friendships, opportunities, and interesting forks in the road are all in front of us, available when we want them. It's up to us to decide if we're going to ignore them or not.

This collection includes essays that document my journey from those days to now in the hopes that they inspire you to go after your own personal goals (while occasionally stopping to smell the roses/hem your pants/buy new shoes/throw out your sweatpants).

One particular essay in this book, "Glitter Matters," represents a criminal investigation. I write mysteries, so I have a natural interest in detection (and can possibly tolerate slightly more details about murder investigations than others), but this case struck me not only for the brilliance and determination of the investigators, but because the clue that led the detectives to the killer was glitter.

Glitter.

It's sparkly and twinkly and girly and remarkably stubborn. Once you introduce glitter into your life—in eyeshadow, party decorations, holiday ornaments, or whatever your reason—you can't ever quite make it go away. In the investigation of the murder of Megan Barroso, the glitter made a difference. There's enough cutthroat competition and keeping up with the Joneses in the world. We could all sparkle, twinkle, and be remarkably stubborn just a little more when it comes to what we want out of life. And that can only separate us from the pack.

Glitter matters.

Reading over these essays, I can see that sometimes I was in too much of a rush to arrive at my destination. Sometimes I was too eager to prove my worth.

But there are other essays that remind me how much control we all have over our lives. How we can rewrite our futures. Nothing is set in stone. We can turn our backs on our critics. We can reinvent into something new. We can wear our flaws and mistakes like badges of honor and keep getting up when we fall down.

I'm closer to my dreams than I was when I started. And as long as I keep moving forward, I'll get there. Armed with determination, drive, and a little bit of glitter. If you ask nicely, I'll share.

xo,

Diane

P.S. A note about reviews: please consider leaving a review for this book. Your review will help other readers discover it and make positive changes in their own lives. No matter how brief or how long, reader reviews make a difference. Thank you!

About The Author

Diane Vallere is a national bestselling author and the creative director of Weekly Diva. Ten years ago, she walked away from a lucrative career at a luxury retailer to follow her dreams. Twenty-five books later, she continues to entertain through her many mystery series. She is passionate about fresh starts, and her mission is to inspire women to put themselves first . . . at least once a week.

Sign up to receive Diane's newsletter, The Weekly DiVa. You'll receive girl talk, book talk, and life talk. Get notice of new books, contests and giveaways, inside stories, and chances to contribute to books in progress: https://dianevallere.com/weekly-diva

Acknowledgments

Acknowledgements for a book like this could easily turn into a laundry list of every person who ever made me stop and think about life differently. And when you consider the impact unexpected celebrities had on individual essays, you realize that laundry list could be a little odd!

But did Donny Osmond or William Shatner tell me to write this book? No. What they did, what my best friend and my flute teacher and my retail buying mentors and my critics did was make me consider things from a different point of view. They made me understand how much control I have—we all have—and how to use that to create the life we want.

I want to thank the people who live unapologetically and authentically. I want to thank the cheerleaders of the world (interestingly, you don't need to audition to become a cheerleader after high school) and the people who constantly say, "why can't you?" instead of "you can't." Most of all, I want to thank you. You've had as much of an impact on me as I hope to have on you, and for that, I am grateful.

www.ingramcontent.com/pod-product-compliance
Lightning Source LLC
Chambersburg PA
CBHW052131110526
44591CB00012B/1678